This book is to be returned on or before
the last date stamped below.

STRATHCLYDE EDUCATION — AYR

Education Resource Service

937

EVANS BROTHERS LIMITED

Evans Brothers Limited
2A Portman Mansions
Chiltern Street
London W1M 1LE

First Published 1994

Printed in Spain by GRAFO, S.A. – Bilbao

ISBN 0 237 51223 8

Acknowledgements

The author and publishers would like to thank the following people for their valuable help and advice:

Dr Simon Esmonde-Cleary PhD, Department of Ancient History and Archaeology, The University of Birmingham

Andrew Selkirk and "Current Archaeology"

Margaret Sharman, author and archaeologist

Verulamium Museum, St Albans, Herts

Illustrations: Jeffery Burn pages 13 and 31
                     Virginia Gray pages 18,19,36-37
Maps: Jillie Luff, Bitmap Graphics

Editor: Jean Coppendale
Design: Neil Sayer
Production: Jenny Mulvanny

For permission to reproduce copyright material the author and publishers gratefully acknowledge the following:

Cover photograph: The Colosseum, Rome. H. Rooney, Trip

Title page: Mosaic showing a sea god or Cernannos, god of the forest. He is seen with lobster claws or antlers coming from his head. Verulamium Museum, St Albans
page 6 Norman Tomalin, Bruce Coleman Limited **page 8** Michael Holford **page 9** (left) Laurence Hughs, The Image Bank, (right) Michael Holford **page 10** (top) e.t. archive, (bottom) Michael Holford **page 11** (middle) Michael Holford, (bottom) e.t. archive, (right) Michael Holford **page 12** (top) e.t. archive, (bottom) Werner Forman Archive, Capitoline Museum, Rome **page 14** Michael Holford **page 15** (top) e.t. archive, (bottom) CM Dixon **page 16** Bridgeman Art Library **page 17** (top) CM Dixon, (middle)
Michael Holford, (bottom right) Peter Clayton **page 19** John G. Ross, Robert Harding Picture Library **page 20** e.t. archive **page 21** Ron Cartmell, Bruce Coleman Limited **page 22** (top) English Heritage Photographic Library, (middle left) e.t. archive, (middle right) Michael Holford, (bottom) CM Dixon **page 23** (middle right) Society of Antiquaries, (bottom left) Robert Harding Picture Library, (bottom right) Museum of Antiquities **page 24** Scala **page 25** (middle left) Robert Harding Picture Library, (middle right) e.t. archive, (bottom) Scala **page 26** (top) e.t. archive, (bottom) Melinda Berge, Bruce Coleman Limited **page 27** (top) Melinda Berge, Bruce Coleman Limited, (middle and bottom) Werner Forman Archive **page 28** (top) Werner Forman Archive, (middle) Michael Holford, (bottom) Verulamium Museum, St Albans **page 29** (left) e.t. archive, (right) Michael Holford **page 30** (top) Brian Philp, (bottom) J.E. Stevenson, Robert Harding Picture Library **page 31** (left) H. Rooney, Trip, (right) Tim Fisher, Life File **page 32** (top) Museo Archeologico Nazionale, Werner Forman Archive, (bottom) Museum of London **page 33** (top) Peter Clayton, (bottom) Shrewsbury Museums **page 34** (top) e.t. archive, (middle) The British Museum, (bottom) Museum of London **page 35** (middle) e.t. archive, (bottom left) Sonia Halliday Photographs, (bottom right) The British Museum **page 36** Michael Holford **page 37** Peter Clayton **page 38** (top) Michael Holford, (middle) Sonia Halliday Photographs, (bottom) Robert Harding Picture Library **page 39** (top) e.t. archive, (middle) The British Museum, (bottom) Michael Holford **page 40** (top) The Bridgeman Art Library, (bottom) Michael Holford **page 41** (top) Peter Clayton, (middle left) e.t. archive, (bottom left) Sonia Halliday Photographs, (right) Topham Picture Source **page 42** (top) Michael Holford, (bottom left) Peter Clayton, (bottom right) Adam Woolfitt, Robert Harding Picture Library **page 43** Peter Clayton **page 44** (top) Verulamium Museum, St Albans, (middle left) York Archaeological Trust, (bottom) e.t. archive **page 45** (top) Verulamium Museum, St Albans, (bottom) University of Cambridge Committee for Aerial Photography

Contents

TIMELINE OF ANCIENT ROME

and the rest of the world

563 BC	Birth of Buddha
551 BC	Birth of Confucius
500 BC	Persian empire at its height
400 BC	Athens became the leading town in Greece
330s BC	Alexander the Great rises to power
214 BC	Great Wall of China finished
AD 0/0 BC	Birth of Jesus Christ
AD 30	Jesus Christ crucified
AD 300	Mayan Empire begins in Central America
AD 449	Angles, Saxons and Jutes begin conquest of Britain
AD 793	Viking raids begin in Europe
AD 900s	Inca Empire expands in Peru

800 BC

700 BC

600 BC

500 BC

400 BC

300 BC

200 BC

100 BC

0 BC

AD 0

AD 100

AD 200

AD 300

AD 400

AD 500

AD 600

AD 700

AD 800

AD 900

AD 1000

	753 BC	Traditional date for the founding of Rome by Romulus and Remus. Greeks colonize parts of southern Italy and Sicily.
	FROM 700 BC	Many different groups of people lived in Italy at this time, such as Etruscans and Latins.
	FROM 600 BC	The emergence of the town of Rome, from villages built on seven nearby hills.
THE ROMAN REPUBLIC 509 BC to 27 BC	509 BC	The last Etruscan king of Rome was overthrown. Roman Republic formed.
	387 BC	Rome invaded by Gauls from the north.
	264 BC	Rome became the leading town in Italy.
	264 to 146 BC	Wars between Rome and Carthage, a city in north Africa.
	73 to 71 BC	A slaves' revolt threatened Rome but was defeated.
	44 BC	Julius Caesar assassinated.
THE ROMAN EMPIRE 27 BC to AD 476	27 BC	Augustus becomes the first Roman emperor. Roman Empire formed.
	AD 64	Fire destroys a large part of Rome.
	AD 79	Mount Vesuvius destroys Pompeii and Herculaneum.
	AD 117	Roman Empire reaches its greatest extent under Emperor Trajan.
	AD 122	Rome builds frontiers at edges of the empire (such as Hadrian's Wall in Britain).
	AD 284	Emperor Diocletian divides the Roman Empire into a western half and an eastern half.
	AD 300 to 500	Barbarian invaders enter the Roman Empire.
	AD 313	Emperor Constantine accepts Christianity.
	AD 324	Emperor Constantine reunites the two parts of the empire.
	AD 330	City of Constantinople (Istanbul) founded.
	AD 395	Roman Empire divided back into two parts.
	AD 410	Rome captured by the Visigoths.
	AD 476	The last Roman emperor is overthrown. End of the Roman Empire in the west.

Dates

Roman history is usually divided into two periods called the 'Republic' and the 'Empire'. The usual way of writing dates is to refer to events before and after the birth of Jesus Christ. Anything before is said to be 'BC' (Before Christ), and anything after is 'AD' (Anno Domini, which is Latin meaning 'in the year of Our Lord').

WHO WERE THE ROMANS?

Introduction to Ancient Rome

The story of Ancient Rome is about one of the most exciting civilizations ever to have existed. When people find out that I am Dr Indiana Jones, the archaeologist, it's not long before they ask if I've been to the Colosseum in Rome, seen the buried Roman town of Pompeii, or Hadrian's Wall in northern England! These are some of the most popular tourist sites of the Roman world, but to really understand what it was like to live in Roman times you have to see a lot more than this!

My university granted me a study trip abroad, and I decided to tour the lands that the Romans knew. I filled many notebooks and took plenty of photographs in the course of my trip. All would come in useful for lectures to my students. And if they didn't take their own notes from my talks, they could always buy my latest book on the Romans – I might even autograph it for them!

A Greek temple built about 450 BC at Paestum, on the west coast of Italy. The Greek name for the city was Poseidonia and the Romans later called it Paestum. The Greeks who settled at Paestum came from Sybaris, about 110 kilometres to the south east. Sybaris was another Greek city in Italy. The finest remains of Greek architecture anywhere in Italy are at Paestum. The Lucanians, a group of people who lived in the south of Italy, eventually took control of Paestum from the Greeks and in AD 273 the city became a Roman colony.

Fact File

People of Ancient Italy

Farmers had lived in Italy from about 6,000 BC (8,000 years ago). When news of Italy's rich farmland spread, people began to migrate there from many parts of Europe. By about 700 BC (2,700 years ago) many different groups of people lived in Italy. In the south, and on the island of Sicily, there were colonists from Greece. The interior of the country was settled by groups such as the Bruttians, Lucanians, Samnites, Latins, Sabines, Umbrians and, most influential of them all, the Etruscans (see page 10). Gradually, one group grew strong enough to control the whole of Italy – the Latins, whose capital was Rome.

Italy

Above   A street in the Roman town of Pompeii.
Above left   A busy street in modern Rome.

N

Alps

R. Po

Ravenna

UMBRIANS

ETRUSCANS
Etruria

Adriatic Sea

Corsica

Tyrrhenian Sea

SABINES
R. Tiber

Cerveteri

Rome

Ostia

LATINS
Latium

SAMNITES

Battle of Cannae
216 BC

Herculaneum

Mt Vesuvius

Pompeii

Sardinia

Paestum

LUCANIANS

Sybaris

Mediterranean

MAGNA GRAECIA

BRUTTIANS

Sea

Sicily

0   km   200
0   miles   100

Map of Italy showing the places
mentioned in this book. This map also
shows the areas where the Etruscans
lived and where Greek colonists settled.
The large Greek-speaking part of Italy is
sometimes called 'Magna Graecia' which
is Latin for 'Greater Greece'.

LATINS   Name of an early
group of people

Area where Latins
and Etruscans lived

Site of battle

The Etruscan civilization

For the first part of my trip I travelled to central Italy, to the homeland of the Etruscans. The Etruscan civilization lasted for about 600 years, from about 700 BC to 100 BC. The Ancient Greeks called them Tyrrhenians, a name which we use today for the sea to the west of their land. The Romans knew them as Tusci or Etrusci. Our modern name for the region in which they lived is Tuscany. Can you see where we get this name from? We believe the Etruscans' own name for themselves was Rasna.

The Etruscans became wealthy by trading not only with other people in Italy, but especially with the Ancient Greeks. The Etruscans had settled in a land that was rich in metal ores and

Inside a painted Etruscan tomb. The tomb was made to look like the inside of a house. This helps us to understand how Etruscan houses may have looked. The painting shows people at a banquet.

▼ This is an elaborate coffin for an Etruscan woman called Seianti who died about 150 BC (her name is written in Etruscan in the bottom right-hand corner of the coffin). She is shown reclining on a couch. When experts examined her skeleton they found that she suffered from arthritis of the jaw and had lost at least 20 teeth. They think she also had dental disease and bad breath!

timber, both of which they exported in return for finished goods, such as fine pottery from Greece.

Much of what we know about the Etruscan civilization has come from excavating their rich cemeteries. At Cerveteri, an Etruscan town about 70 kilometres northwest of Rome, I was able to judge this for myself as I walked among the large, round mounds in the city's ancient burial ground. These were the tombs of Cerveteri's noble and wealthy families. The dead had been buried with valuable gifts for the next life and since the 1830s this cemetery has been giving up its hidden secrets – to both archaeologists and illegal treasure hunters. The Italians call treasure hunters 'clandestini' – but I'd call them thieves and robbers!

Fact File

Etruscan language and writing

The Etruscan language is a great puzzle because it is not like any other language from ancient Europe. This makes it difficult to understand, even though we can recognize all the signs in its alphabet. About 13,000 short inscriptions written in Etruscan have been found. The Etruscan alphabet was taken from one developed by the Phoenicians. Like them, the Etruscans also wrote from right to left. Because the Romans learned their alphabet from the Etruscans, it is perhaps the greatest gift they received from them.

An Etruscan model of an archer on horseback, made of bronze. When new, the metal would have been yellow in colour but after a long time buried in the ground bronze turns green.

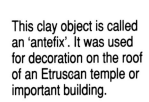

This clay object is called an 'antefix'. It was used for decoration on the roof of an Etruscan temple or important building.

The Etruscans were skilled in working with gold to make jewellery and objects such as this cup.

The rise of Rome

A pottery vessel made in the shape of an early house.

I usually describe the rise of Rome as if it was a tug-of-war contest, with the young superpower-to-be winning some tugs but losing others as the city struggled to become the leader of the whole of Italy.

Rome began in a very small way, starting as a cluster of simple farming villages built on the tops of seven hills in the region known as Latium. The people who lived in Latium were known as Latins. By 600 BC (2,600 years ago) the villages had joined together to become the main city of Latium, with its own temples and public buildings. It is from this point onwards that we can trace the real development of the city of Rome.

For a time Rome was ruled by the powerful Etruscans from the north (see page 10) but the city's population was made up of Latin-speaking people from Latium. As Rome developed, these people grew stronger and they drove out the Etruscans. The traditional date for the overthrow of Tarquin the Proud, the last Etruscan king in Rome, is 509 BC. From then on Rome became an independent state which the Romans called 'respublica', from which we get our word 'republic'. In a republic a group of officials is elected to run a country – not just one person.

Romulus and Remus

A legend tells of the founding of Rome. Twin baby boys called Romulus and Remus were thrown into the River Tiber by Amulius, their wicked great-uncle. Their cradle was washed up at a place near seven hills. A she-wolf found the babies and cared for them until a shepherd took them and brought them up as his own children. When they grew up, they learned how they had been abandoned by Amulius and with the help of local people they overthrew his city. They decided to build their own city on one of the seven hills, but couldn't agree which hill to choose. They argued and Romulus killed Remus. So, Romulus was left to build his city where he wished and it was named Rome after him. The traditional date given for the founding of Rome is 21 April, 753 BC.

This bronze statue of a wolf represents the she-wolf that, according to legend, suckled Romulus and Remus. It was made by an Etruscan artist about 500 BC (2,500 years ago). Although the twins are modern figures (added about AD 1500) it is likely there would have been similar figures in Roman times, but the original ones have not survived.

Early Rome was little more than a group of farming villages built on seven flat-topped hills. Each hill had its own name (see page 15). This reconstruction shows how the first village houses in the region may have looked, about 750 BC (2,750 years ago).

13

THE WORLD OF THE ROMANS

The Romans unite Italy

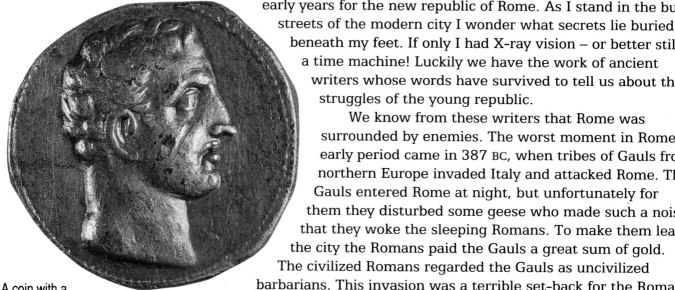

A coin with a portrait of the Carthaginian general, Hannibal. In the war against Rome he was away from his home city of Carthage for almost 35 years, most of the time fighting in Italy.

It's so hard to imagine what it must have been like during those early years for the new republic of Rome. As I stand in the busy streets of the modern city I wonder what secrets lie buried beneath my feet. If only I had X-ray vision – or better still, a time machine! Luckily we have the work of ancient writers whose words have survived to tell us about the struggles of the young republic.

We know from these writers that Rome was surrounded by enemies. The worst moment in Rome's early period came in 387 BC, when tribes of Gauls from northern Europe invaded Italy and attacked Rome. The Gauls entered Rome at night, but unfortunately for them they disturbed some geese who made such a noise that they woke the sleeping Romans. To make them leave the city the Romans paid the Gauls a great sum of gold. The civilized Romans regarded the Gauls as uncivilized barbarians. This invasion was a terrible set-back for the Romans and it was several years before they rebuilt Rome. But when they did they put a strong wall around the city's seven hills: they weren't going to be caught out again!

From this point onwards the Romans planned to be the strongest people in the whole of Italy. For nearly 75 years they fought their enemies in the surrounding areas. Gradually local

Hannibal's march to Italy

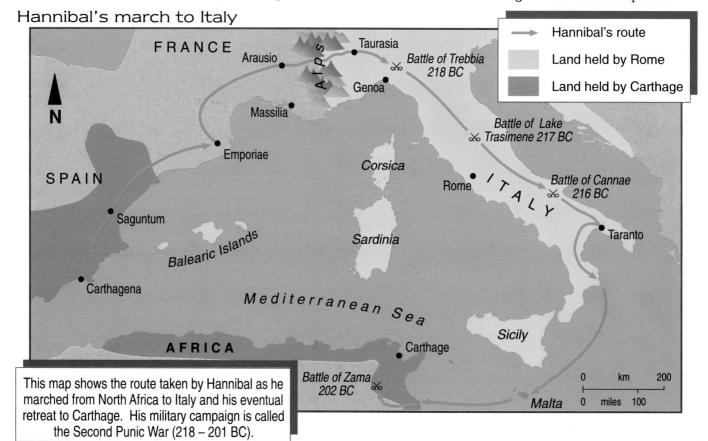

This map shows the route taken by Hannibal as he marched from North Africa to Italy and his eventual retreat to Carthage. His military campaign is called the Second Punic War (218 – 201 BC).

The seven hills of Rome

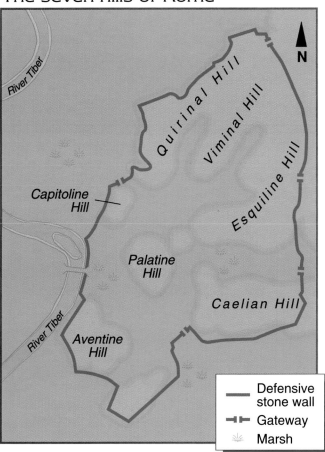

◀ This map shows the seven hills of Rome and the defensive stone wall built around them following the destruction of the city by the barbarian Gauls in 387 BC. The wall, built about 380 BC, allowed entry to the city through five gateways.

This coin shows a war elephant from Hannibal's army. The Romans learned to cope with charging elephants by simply opening ranks to let them pass through. Elephants did not play a great part in the war between the two sides.

tribes came under Roman control and even the mighty Greek colonies in the south of the country could not resist the growing strength of the Romans. By 264 BC their plan had worked. The Romans had become the strongest force in Italy, and Rome was the most important town.

A dagger (with its scabbard) used by the Gauls against the Romans.

Fact File

Hannibal – enemy of Rome

In 241 BC Rome gained control of Sicily from Carthage, a powerful city in North Africa. Hannibal, a Carthaginian general, decided to punish Rome. In 218 BC he led an army from North Africa to Spain, across the Pyrenees, and over the snow-covered Alps. About 20,000 foot soldiers, 6,000 cavalry and 12 war elephants survived the long march to fight the Romans in Italy. At the battle of Cannae in 216 BC about 50,000 Romans were killed – the worst defeat in Rome's entire history. The Romans found a leader to match Hannibal, a general called Scipio. He forced Hannibal back to Africa where he defeated him at the battle of Zama in 202 BC. Then, about 50 years later the Romans destroyed Carthage itself. Its buildings were pulled down and the ground sown with salt so that nothing would grow there again. The wars between Carthage and Rome are called the Punic Wars (Punic is from a Latin word meaning 'Phoenician', for the people who lived in Carthage).

Julius Caesar, the conquering general

One of the first Romans I ever heard about was Julius Caesar. He seems to have had almost as many adventures as me!

Julius Caesar was born in 100 BC in Rome. He came from a leading Roman family and when he was only 20 years old he won the army's top honour for saving the life of a comrade during a battle in Asia. He returned to Rome where he made a name for himself as a great speaker. He became popular with both the senators and the ordinary citizens of Rome. Once, on a trip to the Greek island of Rhodes, he was captured by pirates and only released after a ransom was paid. He later returned to Rhodes, caught the pirates and had them executed.

In 60 BC Caesar was elected consul – the most important job in the Roman Republic (see page 19). It was from this point that Caesar's military career really began. In 58 BC he took charge of the Roman army in Gaul (a large area covering present-day France and Belgium). The tribes in this area were defeated. Then in 55 and 54 BC he invaded southern Britain – but his stay there was short. He had to return to Gaul to stop a rebellion amongst the tribes. Then news reached Caesar that Pompey, another Roman general, was plotting against him in Rome.

In 49 BC Caesar returned to Rome and was made welcome by the people. Pompey fled to Egypt where he was murdered. Caesar was popular with the people and he was declared 'Dictator of Rome'. This made him very powerful – but it also made him many enemies. Some senators feared he was becoming too powerful and their fear led them to assassinate him on 15 March, 44 BC.

For several years after Julius Caesar's death there was disorder in Rome. Peace was eventually restored to the city by Caesar's nephew, Augustus, who became the first Roman emperor (see page 18).

A bronze statue of Julius Caesar dressed in the uniform of a military leader. Under his leadership Roman territory expanded. Caesar was popular with the army and the people, but not with the senators – they plotted his murder.

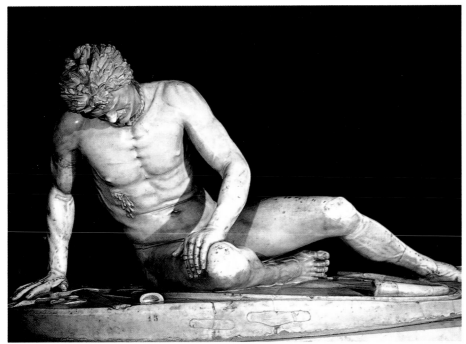

A marble statue known as the 'Dying Gaul', made by the Romans in honour of a victory over the Gauls of northern Europe.

Fact File

The Roman calendar

Did you know that our calendar of 365 days in a year is based on one created by Julius Caesar? He introduced his calendar in 46 BC to replace one that had only 355 days in a year. Under the old system there were still 12 months in the year, but four months had 31 days (March, May, July and October), one had 28 (February) and the rest had 29. To keep the calendar in time with the solar year (which means that mid-summer's day would always fall on the same day each year), the Romans had to have an extra month of 22 or 23 days every other year. It became so confusing that to make the new calendar work, Caesar had to extend the year 46 BC by 90 days!

In the Roman calendar some days were given special names. The 15 March, the day of Caesar's murder, was known as the 'Ides of March'. This coin shows the daggers that stabbed Caesar and the EID MAR inscription refers to the 'Ides of March'.

A portrait of Julius Caesar on a coin. His coins were the first ones to show a portrait of a living Roman. The inscription reads 'CAESAR: DICT PERPETUO' which means 'Caesar, Dictator for Life'. He is shown wearing a wreath of laurel leaves which was a symbol of victory and peace.

Republic and empire

This is the title of a lesson I give to my students. In this lesson I try and condense over 1,000 years of Roman history into less than one hour – I call it 'microwaving history' because I have so much to get through in so little time!

The Roman Republic (509 to 27 BC)

At first Rome was a monarchy ruled by a king. But in 509 BC Rome changed from a monarchy to a republic. The Roman Republic lasted for almost 500 years. Being a republic meant that no individual had too much power, unlike when the Romans were ruled by a king. The most important people in the Roman Republic were two men called 'consuls'. They kept their jobs for one year at a time. By having regular elections different people could become one of the consuls each year. The consuls were advised by experienced politicians called 'senators'. There were about 600 senators – mostly rich men from powerful Roman families. The group of senators was called the Senate and it made important decisions on political, military and legal matters. The Senate became Rome's government. This system worked well in the time of the Roman Republic but it lost much of its power during the Roman Empire when emperors took more and more control.

Roman citizens were divided into 'patricians' (rich men such as nobles) and 'plebeians' (poor men such as farmers and shopkeepers).

This bundle of rods containing an axe, tightly bound with a red strap, was called a 'fasces'. It was an ancient sign of authority, first used by the Etruscans. Later, Rome's early kings adopted it and during the Roman Republic the consuls took turns to hold the 'fasces'.

The Roman Empire (27 BC to AD 476)

During the time of the Roman Republic, Roman armies conquered lands throughout Europe, Africa and the Middle East. Between 100 BC and 50 BC civil wars broke out with Romans fighting Romans. With strong generals at the head of the army the Roman senators thought that one of them wanted to become king. They feared Julius Caesar the most and had him murdered (see page 16). But this terrible act only caused more fighting. It was Caesar's nephew, Octavian, who finally restored law and order to Rome, and in 27 BC he became the first Roman emperor – a king by another name. He is better known as Augustus, the title he was given. In the 500 years of the Roman Empire, Rome had nearly 100 emperors.

This is how a Roman army standard may have looked. A standard was an important symbol. To lose one was a disgrace. The letters SPQR were a Latin abbreviation for 'Senatus Populus Que Romanus', which meant 'The Senate and the People of Rome'. The decorations on a standard were awarded for battle victories and bravery.

Gaius Julius Caesar Octavianus, better known as Rome's first emperor, Augustus. The rod in his left hand is an army standard which the Romans had lost in battle. Augustus succeeded in recovering it and that event is shown on his finely carved breastplate. Statues of Augustus were set up all over the Roman Empire.

The Roman Empire

In AD 113 a war memorial was erected in Rome to commemorate Emperor Trajan's victory over the Dacians (in modern day Romania). Known as 'Trajan's Column' it is 30 metres high (see page 6) and is decorated with carvings that run in a spiral. The carvings tell how Trajan conquered the Dacians, as in this detail where people take cover inside a fort. If the spiral was unwound, the carvings would form a picture about 200 metres long!

On my trip I had with me a map of the Roman Empire which showed just how much land the Romans had conquered. I placed it over a modern map and could see that the total amount of land they controlled in Europe, Asia and Africa has never been bettered – before or since! I wonder how much further they might have gone if they had had transport like our own?

It was after the Romans had become the most powerful people in Italy that they began to add foreign lands to their territory. From then on their empire began to grow. In 146 BC the Carthaginians were defeated and Rome took over all their land in North Africa and the Mediterranean (see page 15). In the same year Greece came under Roman control. Not every land was conquered by force. Some countries asked Rome to help them settle disputes. In return they promised to obey Rome. Other countries became part of the Roman Empire when their rulers gave them to Rome, as happened with some lands in the Middle East. The Romans used the word 'provincia' to describe their foreign lands, from which our own word 'province' comes.

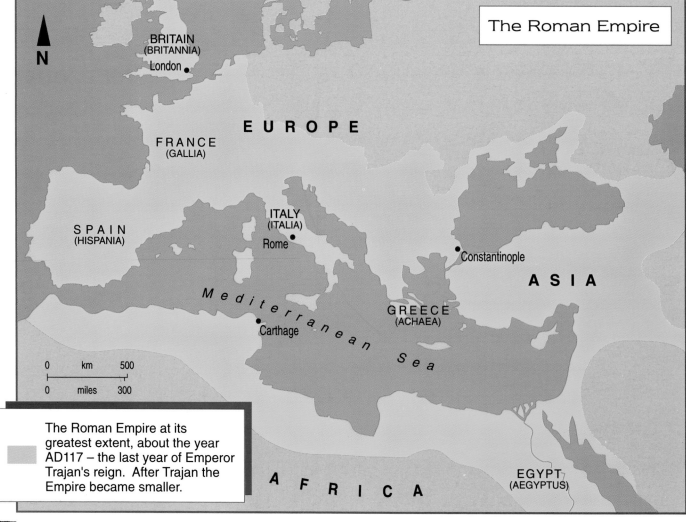

The Roman Empire

N

BRITAIN (BRITANNIA)
London

EUROPE

FRANCE (GALLIA)

SPAIN (HISPANIA)

ITALY (ITALIA)
Rome

Constantinople

ASIA

Mediterranean Sea

GREECE (ACHAEA)

Carthage

0   km   500
0   miles   300

EGYPT (AEGYPTUS)

AFRICA

The Roman Empire at its greatest extent, about the year AD117 – the last year of Emperor Trajan's reign. After Trajan the Empire became smaller.

In AD 118 a revolt amongst the northern tribes in Britain was stopped by the Romans. In AD 122 Emperor Hadrian called for a stone and turf wall to be built to protect Roman Britain from the trouble-makers in the north. Parts of it were painted white so it could be seen from a distance. Hadrian's Wall became the northern boundary of the Roman Empire for 250 years. It ran for 120 kilometres and crossed the country from coast to coast.

The Roman Empire was at its most extensive in the reign of Emperor Trajan who was emperor from AD 98 to AD 117. But having a great empire had its problems. It was expensive to control and look after so many provinces. Soldiers had to be stationed abroad in case a province rebelled – and the soldiers had to be paid. Expensive roads and bridges had to be built. Even though taxes were collected from the provinces it was often not enough to meet the costs of actually looking after them. Rome found itself under more and more pressure and just over 100 years after Trajan had increased the empire to its greatest extent, it began to break up (see page 42).

Fact File

Goods from the Empire

The Roman Empire was rich in goods that Rome wanted and valuable supplies were taken to Rome from distant lands. This meant that exotic and rare produce could be enjoyed by wealthy Romans. Here are some of the goods sent to Rome, and the areas from which they came.

Goods	Land
Gold	Balkans, Spain, Wales
Grain	Egypt, Spain, North Africa
Honey	Spain
Horses	Spain
Lead	Britain
Marble	Greece, Turkey, North Africa
Olive oil	Greece, Spain, Turkey, North Africa
Papyrus	Egypt
Perfume	Asia
Pottery	France, Greece, Spain
Silk	China
Slaves	Britain, Germany, Greece, Turkey
Spices	Asia
Timber	Germany
Tin	Britain
Wine	France, Spain, Middle East

Ancient Rome at war

Housesteads Fort, where soldiers who patrolled Hadrian's Wall in northern Britain were stationed. You can see the remains of the fort's buildings – its headquarters, commander's house, barracks, granaries, hospital, toilets and gateways.

In Rome I stood in front of Trajan's Column and peered up at its carvings (see pages 6 and 20). I could see how the Romans had pictured themselves – as well-armed, well-organized fighters. Another way of finding out about the Roman army at war is by reading accounts actually written at the time. Julius Caesar, a famous Roman general (see page 16) described how his army attacked a tribe in northern Europe. He wrote, 'Our soldiers cleared a way by using slings, arrows and war engines. This helped our troops.

How a Roman ▶ legionary soldier dressed. His body and shoulders were protected by plates of steel armour and he wore a steel helmet which gave good protection to his head and neck. His kilt was formed from leather strips covered with metal, and on his feet were thick-soled leather sandals. When he was on the march he carried food, tools and even cooking equipment.

▲
The soldiers in this mosaic picture have shields for defence and javelins for attack.

When advancing, soldiers covered themselves with their shields. This formation was called a 'testudo' or tortoise.

They made a mass charge and made the enemy run away.' I certainly know which side I would have been on!

The Romans needed a large army to protect their empire from attackers – both from outside the empire and from rebellions within it. All men who were Roman citizens aged between 17 and 46 could be called on to join the army. They joined large army units called 'legions', and the soldiers themselves were called 'legionaries'. Each legion had about 5,300 foot soldiers, divided into ten smaller units called 'cohorts'. Even smaller units were called 'centuries' which had 80 men in them (at first they had 100 men each). The smallest units had eight men each – the so-called 'tent-parties'. These were groups who shared tents and sleeping quarters together.

Men from the Roman provinces, and who were therefore not classed as Roman citizens, could also join the army. They were called 'auxiliaries' and their numbers made up almost half the army. After they had completed their military service they were granted Roman citizenship, which was very precious to them.

Soldiers joined the army for 25 years and in all that time they could not marry. On leaving the army they were given some land on which they could start a small farm.

A Roman helmet with a face mask like this was not worn in battle. It would have been worn on special occasions only, such as parades.

Fact File

Heavy weapons

Just like a modern army, there were surprises in store for an unsuspecting, and unfortunate, enemy! The 'carroballista' and the 'onager' were two kinds of heavy weapon. Both were operated by strong springs. The 'carroballista' could be mounted on a cart, pulled by two ponies. Ten men were needed to fire the weapon which shot long-range arrows or iron bolts deep behind enemy lines. The 'onager' was a catapult that could hurl large boulders over a great distance. Weapons such as these were used to weaken an enemy before any hand-to-hand fighting began.

The head of an iron bolt fired from a powerful Roman weapon called a 'carroballista', a type of crossbow. It was found lodged in the spine of a man who had died defending a British community from a Roman attack.

This model shows how an 'onager' probably looked. It could throw large rocks over long distances and was used during sieges. Its name means 'wild ass' after the kicking action when it was fired.

Rome – capital of the empire

How Rome may have looked in AD 300. Visitors would have been impressed by its magnificent public buildings – but they would not have seen its slums where most of the population lived.

As I walked among the ruins of ancient Rome, I remembered the saying, 'Rome wasn't built in a day'. It means that to do anything well you must have lots of patience – or power. It also refers to the grandeur created by Rome's early emperors. Emperor Augustus, the first emperor (see page 19) said, 'I found Rome a city of bricks but I left it a city of marble'. How right he was! If I can be impressed just by the sight of fragments of the ancient city, what must it have looked like nearly 2,000 years ago?

For an idea of how Rome looked then, look at the picture on this page. The model shows Rome at its grandest, about the year AD 200, when one million people lived there. With its network of roads, its groups of houses and its large, important buildings, it had all the features of a successful city – and many of the problems, too. There was poverty and many ordinary citizens lived in awful conditions. Successive Roman emperors had built larger and grander buildings but neglected to build better housing for the poor. Greedy landlords took advantage of this situation. They built extra floors on the houses they owned and squeezed even more people inside. More people meant more rent for the owners. This type of housing resembled small blocks of flats – but without

any running water, no toilets and with little natural light.

To me, ancient Rome was a city of contrasts – like many cities in the world today. The rich lived well and enjoyed the benefits of being in the capital. But for most people life was hard, with a shortage of work, poor living conditions and a short life. You were very old if you reached the age of 50!

Trajan's Market was a large market-place, or 'forum', in the centre of Rome. It had law courts, shops, offices, libraries and meeting rooms.

A model of a block of flats from Ostia, the port of Rome. There were many blocks like this in Rome. The ground floor was filled with shops and the upper storeys provided poor quality, overcrowded housing. For safety reasons they could not be built higher than about 20 metres.

Fact File

Rome on fire

In AD 64 a fire burned for nine days and destroyed a large part of Rome. The emperor at this time was Nero and he may have ordered his servants to start it. Why? Nero wanted a grand palace and after the fire he bought the burnt-out parts of the city. He cleared the land and built a palace which he called the 'Golden House'. It was adorned with gold plate, mother-of-pearl and statues taken from Greek cities. 'I have begun,' he said, 'to be housed as a man ought to be.' When Nero learned that people were saying he had started the fire on purpose, he blamed it on Christians, who were then a new religious sect (see page 40). Many Christians were executed on Nero's orders. He became very unpopular, and faced with a rebellion he committed suicide at the age of 32.

Emperor Nero almost bankrupted Rome with his expensive schemes to rebuild the city after the great fire.

Pompeii – a Roman town

The Romans kept guard dogs, as this mosaic from Pompeii shows. One mosaic even bore the message 'cave canem' which is Latin for beware of the dog!

Pompeii's streets formed a grid pattern of squares and rectangles. Houses and shops were built inside the squares. Each square was called an 'insula', meaning 'island', because it was surrounded by streets. Most Roman towns followed a grid pattern.

To find out about the lives of ordinary Romans I knew I must leave Rome, which was, after all, a 'show-piece' city built by the Roman emperors. Towns in the country would be very different from the capital. I travelled south, about 200 kilometres from Rome, to the small town of Pompeii. I thought I had stepped back 2,000 years when I saw what Pompeii looked like, with its intact houses, shops and streets. And in the distance was the cause of all this incredible preservation – the volcano, Mount Vesuvius. I just hoped that it wouldn't blow its top while I was visiting Pompeii!

On 24 August, AD 79, Mount Vesuvius erupted. The volcano had been quiet for years and the people living in towns nearby could not have expected it to explode with such destructive force. The day had begun as a public holiday but within hours the towns of Pompeii, Herculaneum, Stabiae and Oplontis were destroyed.

Lava pebbles, pumice, ash and poisonous gases rained down on Pompeii, burying the town under about four metres of debris. Of the town's 20,000 inhabitants, about 2,000 were killed. Those that escaped lost all their possessions and were made homeless.

The destruction of Pompeii was a natural disaster, but it has preserved a complete Roman town for archaeologists to study. Not only are buildings preserved, but so are traces of the people who lived and worked in them. We have found the contents of shops, unfinished meals on tables, wall paintings and from seeds found in gardens we can tell what plants the people of Pompeii

▶ A person who died during the eruption of Mount Vesuvius. The body was covered by ash and over the centuries it has vanished, leaving a body-shaped space behind. By pumping plaster of Paris into the space the exact shape of the body can be found.

◀ The street in the left of this picture has a stepping stone in it for pedestrians to use when crossing the road. Wheeled vehicles could pass over the stone. Look for the ruts their wheels have made beyond the stone.

Fact File

Herculaneum

Herculaneum was a Roman seaside town near Mount Vesuvius, about 16 kilometres away from Pompeii. Some of Rome's leading families had luxurious houses there where they went for holidays. When Vesuvius erupted this wealthy town was submerged under 20 metres of hot lava which flowed out of the volcano. It cooled to set as hard as rock. Most of the inhabitants managed to escape – leaving their belongings behind. Herculaneum became a 'time capsule', sealed from the outside world. People forgot about the town until 1709 when a workman digging a well found blocks of marble buried deep under the ground. From this time onwards, Herculaneum has gradually been uncovered and the work still goes on today.

grew. Some of the buildings have graffiti scribbled on their walls. A Roman with a sense of humour wrote on one wall, 'Everyone writes on walls except me!' We have also discovered victims of the eruption buried under the debris from Vesuvius. Although their bodies rotted away long ago their shapes have been preserved as hollow spaces which can be filled with plaster of Paris. When the plaster has set we can remove the volcanic debris to see the ghostly shapes of people and animals just as they were the moment disaster struck.

The Romans didn't use wallpaper, but they did paint the walls of their houses. These paintings are in a house at Pompeii.

Everyday life in towns

At Pompeii I saw for myself what the streets and buildings of a Roman town had looked like. But what sort of lives did people lead in Roman towns?

Most towns were built to the same basic design. At their heart was a large open area called the 'forum'. It was the town's market-place, where traders sold produce and where business people met. Around the sides of the forum were shops and offices. Just like our own markets today, the Roman forum would have been a noisy place, packed with busy people – and bargains if you were lucky! Next door to the forum was the 'basilica', a large public building for the town's officials. It was similar to our present-day town hall.

A vital necessity of town life was the water supply. Without adequate supplies of fresh, clean water, disease could spread quickly in the cramped and dirty conditions. Water was carried into towns by underground pipes and

▲
Most Roman towns had public baths. This example is at Pompeii and was used as a steam room, just like our saunas are today. Hot air circulated under the floor and along channels behind the walls. The temperature was high and a Roman writer said it was 'like being on a bonfire!'

▲
This bronze object, called a 'strigil', was used in Roman baths. Bathers rubbed oil on to their bodies and then scraped it off, with all the dirt, using a strigil.

Pots such as these were used throughout the Roman Empire for carrying wine, oil, honey and for grinding food in. To the left is a pot full of holes for straining liquids.

also by special bridges called 'aqueducts' (see page 30). Wells were dug inside towns. To stop them from drying out they often had to be deepened – a dangerous job for a workman.

At the end of the day some people would go to the town's baths – which to us would be like a mixture between a swimming pool, a sauna and an exercise gym! Inside were three types of bath: cold, warm and hot. The visitor would spend time in each before finishing with a massage. If you wanted to meet friends and catch up on the day's news and gossip, then a trip to the baths was essential!

Meal times were another occasion when friends and family came together. Romans ate their meals reclining on couches – not sitting at tables as we do. Another difference is that they didn't use cutlery – instead they used bread to scoop up their food. An important meal might consist of shellfish, eggs, snails and vegetables, followed by fish and roasted birds. Then came venison, hare, pork and more fish. Finally, many kinds of fruit were served. Wine was drunk with the meal. Guests who had eaten too much could leave the room to be sick – before returning, ready to start eating all over again. This way, a Roman banquet was guaranteed to last a long time! I don't think I'll try this out for myself!

Fact File
Country life

Wealthy Romans often owned a house in a town and one in the country too. The country house was called a 'villa'. But the villa was more than just a second home. It was a farm, with the villa at the centre of an estate. Slaves were used to work the land and their conditions could be hard, especially if they worked for a cruel owner. Some slaves worked for caring masters, and as a reward for good service they might be given their freedom, and so become Roman citizens. Villas and their estates were an essential part of Roman life, since the food they produced was supplied to nearby towns. Cereals, cabbages, lettuces, tomatoes, carrots, olives, apples, figs, pears and grapes were grown. Pork was the most popular meat, so herds of pigs were raised. Sheep were kept for wool and milk, and chickens for eggs and meat. Pigeons were bred for winter meat. The Romans didn't know about sugar, so they used honey instead. You would always see bee hives on a farm estate.

A wall painting of a villa in the countryside.

A mosaic picture of a group of people reclining at a meal while a musician entertains them with music.

ROMAN ACHIEVEMENTS

Roads and buildings

Milestones were placed along roads, giving information about distances between places. One Roman mile measured 1,472 metres (one mile today measures 1,609 metres). This milestone was found on the Fosse Way near Leicester, England. It was erected during the reign of Emperor Hadrian in AD 120.

In Rome I walked with a group of tourists for a while. Sure enough, before long I heard their guide repeat a familiar saying, 'All roads lead to Rome'. I don't think the visitors from Japan and the USA agreed with him! Even so, there was some truth in what he said.

Towns throughout the Roman Empire were connected by a network of roads. It was vital that the road system worked well, otherwise important news could not be passed between places. And as Rome was at the centre of communications for the empire, all roads did lead to it – eventually! In 20 BC Emperor Augustus erected the famous 'golden milestone' in Rome. It was a marble column on to which were fixed golden plates with distances from Rome to towns throughout the empire.

Roads were often built by the army so that soldiers could be moved quickly across new land. Some roads were frontiers marking the new boundaries of the expanding Roman Empire. Gradually, as any danger passed, minor roads were built branching off from the main roads, taking traffic further inland.

Experts believe the Romans built over 90,000 kilometres of road. About 16,000 kilometres were built in Britain alone. Some modern roads are built on top of Roman ones – so we are still using the same routes 2,000 years after the Romans first planned them!

This aqueduct carried drinking water across the River Gard and into the French city of Nîmes. Water flowed inside a channel along the very top of the aqueduct, above the small arches. The word aqueduct comes from the Latin 'aquam ducere' meaning 'to carry water'. Look for the people in the pphotograph to see just how big this aqueduct is.

Fact File

Concrete

If you think concrete is a modern invention, then think again! The Romans combined ash, lime mortar, sand and gravel to produce the first concrete in the world – a waterproof and incredibly hard material. Concrete revolutionized the Roman building industry. Because liquid concrete could be poured into moulds it was possible to cast it into lots of different shapes. Architects were able to design new types of building using concrete and two famous Roman buildings could not have been built without it – the Colosseum (see page 38) and the Pantheon.

Across soft ground

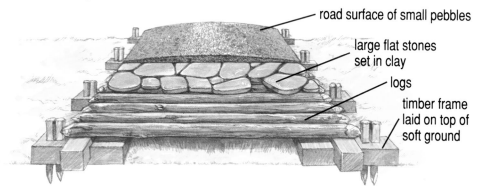

road surface of small pebbles

large flat stones set in clay

logs

timber frame laid on top of soft ground

Across hard ground

road surface of large flat stones set in a 'camber' (curve) so that rainwater could run off into the roadside ditches

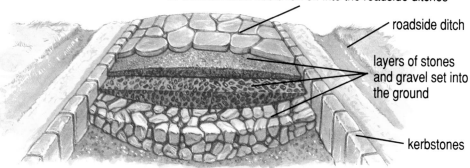

roadside ditch

layers of stones and gravel set into the ground

kerbstones

Cross-sections through two types of Roman road, showing the different methods of building them.

This temple building in Rome is called the Pantheon. It was built about AD 120 and its dome was made from overlapping rings of concrete. The hole at the top of the dome let daylight into the building.

▲
Seen from above, the straightness of a Roman road can really be appreciated. This road is in Wales. Roads like this were plotted by surveyors and wherever possible they took the most direct course between two points – which is why they were so straight.

Language and writing

The language the Romans used was called Latin. In its time Latin was probably the most widely spoken language in the world. A traveller could go from Britain to the Middle East and north Africa, knowing that he could use Latin and be understood. If I used Latin on the same trip today, no one would understand me! Latin is the ancestor of many languages used today, and we can spot similar words in different languages.

How did the Romans write their language down? We know a lot about this because there is much evidence to study. There are literally thousands of inscriptions to read. Some are very impressive and are carved on important buildings, while others are more humble such as ones carved on tombstones or written on personal property. It is often the personal inscriptions that are the most interesting, such as the words 'Faustine vivas' (meaning long live Faustinus) written on a silver spoon found in 1992 amongst a hoard of Roman treasure from Suffolk, England. Experts think it is a reference to the wealthy Faustinus family who lived in that area about 1,500 years ago. From these two Latin words it is possible to link the treasure to a real Roman family – a very rare and exciting event!

This wall painting from Pompeii shows a girl holding a set of wooden writing tablets like the one in the picture below. In her right hand is a writing instrument called a 'stylus'. Note how she holds it.

A collection of Roman writing implements: a wooden tablet which held a thin layer of wax, metal pens for scratching into the wax and two inkwells.

Since 1973 wooden writing tablets have been excavated at Vindolanda, a fort on Hadrian's Wall in northern Britain. Waterlogged soil has preserved the tablets, together with traces of writing which are 1,800 years old. These tablets were written on in ink, not scratched on as with the tablets coated with wax. From them we can learn about life in a fort at the very edge of the Roman Empire.

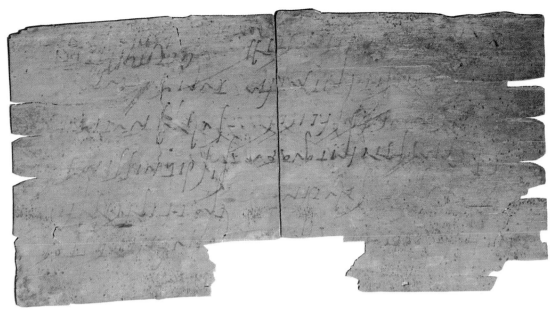

One type of material the Romans wrote on was papyrus – a kind of paper made from layers of reeds. Instead of books with separate pages, the Romans used papyrus rolls. When fully opened the rolls could be several metres long. A finer type of writing material was parchment (also called vellum). This was made from sheep and goat skins. Anything written on papyrus or parchment became a permanent record. For everyday notes and letters the Romans used small tablets of wood, coated with wax. A metal rod called a stylus was used to scratch into the wax. When the message had been read, the blunt end of the stylus smoothed the wax over, and the wax could be written on again.

Fact File

Inscriptions

Roman inscriptions can look like a line of initials, because common words were shortened to abbreviations – often single letters. Names such as Aulus, Quintus and Sextus were abbreviated to A, Q and S. Each letter had its own meaning and to the trained eye can be read quite easily.

Latin abbreviations are still used today. In Britain, for example, the country's coins are minted with the Latin abbreviation 'D.G.REG.F.D'. In full, this stands for 'Dei Gratia Regina Fidei Defensor' which means 'by the grace of God, the Queen, Defender of the Faith'.

Roman cities often had inscriptions carved in stone to record the visit of an emperor or a famous general. This inscription from the city of Viroconium (Wroxeter) in Shropshire, England, refers to the rebuilding of the city during the reign of Emperor Hadrian. Look for his name. It dates from about AD 130 and a master craftsman from Rome may have cut the letters.

Crafts of the Romans

Jewellery

Gold and silver were used for rings, anklets, bracelets, chains, earrings, tiaras and brooches. Both men and women wore rings on their fingers, often between the first and second finger joints, not between the second and third. This explains why Roman rings can be tiny, looking as if they were meant for children rather than adults. Children wore a 'bulla'. This was an ornament around the neck designed to protect them from misfortune.

A gold necklace from Pompeii, decorated with precious stones and mother-of-pearl.

Pottery

Pottery-making was carried out on a large scale, and some areas of the Roman Empire specialized in certain types of pottery. Large, round-bodied pots called amphorae were produced in Spain. These were used to hold wine, olive oil or fish sauce. Red pottery with a shiny surface was made in France. Millions of pieces of this fine tableware were made, some of which were stamped with their potters' names. In Britain, in the area around Oxford, mixing bowls were made from a white clay. Sharp pieces of grit on the inside of the bowls made their surfaces rough for grinding and crushing food. Some of these bowls also had their makers' names stamped on to them.

This brooch is called a cameo. It was made from a semi-precious stone which was carved to reveal the different layers of colour. The cameo shows a portrait of Emperor Augustus.

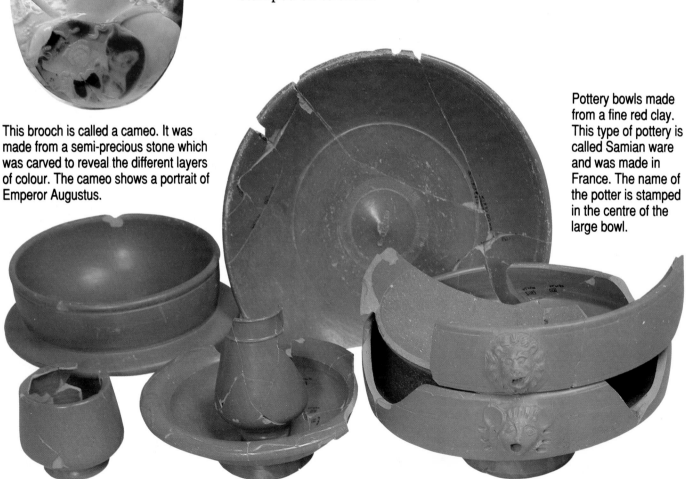

Pottery bowls made from a fine red clay. This type of pottery is called Samian ware and was made in France. The name of the potter is stamped in the centre of the large bowl.

Paintings and mosaics

Roman buildings were often highly decorated on the inside. At Pompeii (see page 26) wall paintings are well preserved and show us that the Romans liked to decorate their rooms with colourful pictures. Mosaics were pictures too, usually on the floor but sometimes on the walls, made from tiny cubes of coloured stone called tesserae. Pieces of pottery or glass were also used in mosaic pictures. Different coloured tesserae were used to make striking, hard-wearing designs.

A wall painting from Pompeii of a man dressed in a toga, the usual one-piece garment worn by Roman men. A helper assisted the wearer to put his toga on. The toga was usually made of uncoloured wool.

Fact File

What did they wear?

The Romans wore different types of clothes in different climates and for various occasions. One of the best known items of Roman clothing was the toga which may have begun with the Etruscans (see page 10), as it was similar to their wrap-around cloak. The toga was at first worn by both Roman men and women, but it seems to have gone out of fashion with women at an early date. Woven from wool, the toga was semi-circular in shape and about five metres long. It was draped over the left shoulder, around the body and then over the right arm. A toga worn by a boy between the ages of 14 and 16 usually had a purple border added to its long straight edge.

The standard garment for a married Roman woman was the 'stola'. This was a long, folded gown, with or without sleeves, which reached to the ground. Brooches fastened the stola to the underclothes. Unmarried women wore a plain tunic.

This mosaic found in Sicily shows young girls exercising in bikinis.

This blue glass vase, coated with carved white glass, was found in a tomb near Rome where it originally held the ashes from a cremation. Today it is known as the Portland Vase, named after the Duke of Portland who once owned it. In 1845 it was smashed to pieces by a visitor to the British Museum – but the repair work is so good you cannot see the joins.

RELIGION AND FESTIVALS

Gods and goddesses

A coin showing the god Janus. He was shown with two faces – one looking back to the old and the other looking forward to the new. The month of January is named after him because it represents the passing of the old year and the start of the new year.

I have heard the religion of the Romans described as 'gods by conquest'. What does this mean? It tells us that the Romans added other peoples' gods to their own religion – so when they conquered a country they also conquered their gods.

Many aspects of Roman life were governed by particular gods. People were superstitious and prayed to the gods for protection and good fortune. Sacrifices of animals, usually cattle, sheep, pigs, goats and doves, were made. Priests killed the animals with special knives, and officials examined the entrails (insides) for signs of good or bad luck. For example, the colour and size of the liver was said to show if the gods were pleased or angry.

With lots of different gods, many festivals to celebrate and with no single god that everyone believed in, Roman religion must have seemed very confusing. When a new religion began in Palestine, in the first century AD, it probably seemed like a local cult that would eventually disappear, as so many others had before it. This religion was called Christianity and rather than disappearing without trace it grew and spread so that by the fourth century AD it became the official religion of the empire, and worship of the old Roman gods was banned (see page 40).

Diana
She was goddess of the moon and hunting.

Vulcan
He was the god of fire and metal-working.

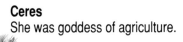

Ceres
She was goddess of agriculture.

Jupiter
He was the king of the gods whose symbol was an eagle.

Fact File

Temples

Roman temples were copied from those of the Ancient Greeks and Etruscans. Rows of columns lined the sides of a temple and inside was a statue of the god whose temple it was. The statue was often covered in gold and jewellery. In the courtyard at the front of the temple was an altar at which sacrifices would be made.

A Roman temple in Nîmes, southern France.

Roman gods and goddesses

This table shows the most important gods and goddesses. Some were taken by the Romans from other religions. For example, the twelve most important gods worshipped by the Ancient Greeks were absorbed into the Roman religion. These Greek gods are marked with an asterisk (*). The Romans gave them new names but mostly left their duties unchanged.

1. Apollo*   god of sun, light and good fortune.
2. Bacchus   god of wine.
3. Ceres*   goddess of agriculture.
4. Diana*   goddess of the moon and hunting.
5. Janus   god of new beginnings – the first hour of the day, the first day of the month, and so on.
6. Jupiter*   god of the sky and king of the gods.
7. Juno*   goddess of marriage and women.
8. Mars*   god of war.
9. Mercury*   god of trade and communications.
10. Minerva*   goddess of art and war.
11. Neptune*   god of the sea.
12. Pluto   god of the underworld.
13. Saturn   god of agriculture.
14. Venus*   goddess of love and beauty.
15. Vesta*   goddess of the family and the hearth.
16. Vulcan*   god of fire and metal-working.

Juno
She was the queen of the gods whose symbols were a peacock and a pomegranate.

Neptune
He was the god of the sea.

Mercury
He was the god of trade and communications.

Games and gladiators

A lightly-armoured gladiator known as a 'retiarius'. He is holding a trident and a short sword.

The Colosseum in Rome is the most famous Roman amphitheatre (see front cover). Its name comes from a huge statue (called a colossus) of the Emperor Nero that once stood nearby. 50,000 spectators filled the Colosseum to watch gladiator fights and animal hunts. The floor of the arena is now missing and you can see the underground passages where gladiators and animals waited before a contest.

The Romans loved to be entertained. We do too, of course, but I don't think Roman entertainment would be to our liking! It's hard to understand how they could enjoy the theatre one day and on another day watch animals being slaughtered or men fight to the death. But to the Romans these spectacles were acceptable. Let's look at three types of shows they enjoyed.

Chariot races

In Rome was the 'Circus Maximus' (this means the Great Circus). This open-air building was an oval racetrack for horse-drawn chariots. It was 600 metres long and had seats for 250,000 spectators. Races were usually seven laps of the track – about eight kilometres. Chariot drivers could earn a lot of money – for themselves and their managers. One charioteer, Diocles, was in 4,257 races in 24 years. He won 1,462 of them!

Gladiator fights

Tough slaves and criminals fought in front of audiences in open-air arenas called amphitheatres. The fighters were called gladiators (this means swordsmen). They were trained to fight in different ways and with different types of equipment. A 'secutor' gladiator had heavy armour and a sword. A lightly-armoured 'retiarius'

gladiator had a net, a trident and a short sword. A 'secutor' usually fought a 'retiarius' – the Romans thought the differences between them made the fight good to watch. Gladiators often fought to the death.

Animal hunts

A fighter who killed wild animals in front of an audience was called a 'bestiarius'. Animals such as elephants, lions, panthers, leopards and boars were caught and taken to Rome. In the city's amphitheatres beast-hunters stalked them as if they were in the wild before killing them.

A mosaic picture of a lion hunt. Exotic animals were caught in the wild and taken to Rome where they were killed in mock hunts in amphitheatres. Wild animals were especially collected in north Africa.

A bronze helmet worn by a 'secutor' gladiator. It protected the head and neck, but its weight slowed the fighter down and made him vulnerable to attack.

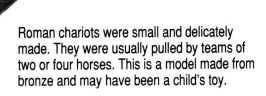

Roman chariots were small and delicately made. They were usually pulled by teams of two or four horses. This is a model made from bronze and may have been a child's toy.

Fact File

Thumbs up or down?

Sometimes a gladiator could appeal to the audience for his life to be spared. This usually only happened if the fight had been a good one and the defeated man had fought well. He appealed to the crowd by raising a finger to them. At this sign the crowd would respond by either giving a 'thumbs pressed' sign (pressing a thumb into the palm of the other hand) or by a 'thumbs turned' sign (pointing a thumb down to the ground). The 'thumbs pressed' sign meant mercy was given, but the 'thumbs turned' sign meant no mercy and the poor man was killed. The thumb may have represented the sword – so touching your palm was indicating the sword should be put back in its sheath, whereas turning it down was like swishing a sword through the air. Our own thumbs up and thumbs down signs (for 'good' and 'bad') may be connected with this Roman tradition.

Christianity

A mosaic picture of Jesus Christ, found in a Roman building in Dorset, England. He is shown dressed in a Roman toga and behind his head is an important symbol used by early Christians. It is an X and P which are the first two letters of Christ's name in Greek. These letters are called 'chi' and 'rho' and so this symbol is called the 'chi-rho' sign.

The Romans usually tolerated 'foreign' religions, so much so that they took over other peoples' gods and worshipped them as their own (see page 36). But there was one religion they found hard to accept – Christianity. This new religion was worshipped by followers of Jesus Christ who had lived and died in the early years of the first century AD in the Roman province of Judaea, an area that covers modern Israel, Palestine and Lebanon.

Why did the Romans fear Christianity? Christians believed in only one god. They did not worship Roman gods and more importantly they did not believe the emperor was a living god. These were seen as signs of rebellion against Rome, and Christians were rounded up and killed – often in front of Roman audiences in amphitheatres where they were savaged by wild animals (see page 38). The Romans could not understand why anyone would want to follow the teachings of Jesus Christ – a man whom they had regarded as a common criminal and whom they had executed. Christianity was banned but its followers found ways of passing on their new religion to others.

Christianity proved to be a strong religion and Roman attempts to wipe it out failed. Rather than disappearing (like other cults had) it spread throughout the Roman Empire. In the fourth century AD, Emperor Constantine accepted that Christianity was going to survive and in AD 313 he made it the official religion of Rome. This meant that after 300 years of persecution, Christians could at last openly follow the teachings of Jesus Christ. Constantine was himself converted to the new faith shortly before he died in AD 337.

After Emperor Constantine allowed Christians to worship their religion openly, many churches were built, some of which are still in use today and have been added to by later Christians. This church was built in the early 500s, in Rome.

A triangular plaque made of silver representing a palm leaf. The 'chi-rho' sign shows its connection with Christianity. It is one of several Christian objects found at a small Roman town in England where they would have been used in religious services.

Helena, mother of Emperor Constantine. She was converted to Christianity and built many churches in Palestine on the sites of holy places. According to tradition, she discovered Christ's cross.

Fact File

The catacombs of Rome

Bodies of poor Romans were usually cremated. But early Christians in Rome preferred to bury their dead. The problem was they could not afford to build cemeteries large enough for their growing numbers. They solved the problem by digging tunnels, called 'catacombs', under Rome's streets. Thousands were buried in the passages, in slots cut into the walls which were then sealed with blocks of stone. There are over 900 kilometres of catacombs in Rome! Other cities also had catacombs. The word 'catacomb' means 'at the hollows' and it comes from a Greek word. The catacombs of Rome went out of use and were forgotten until 1578 when a landslip revealed their presence.

Inside the catacombs of Rome the underground passages are lined with niches cut into the walls. Bodies were buried in these slots and blocks of stone sealed the niches after use.

A portrait of the Emperor Constantine on a gold coin. He was responsible for the acceptance of Christianity by the Romans.

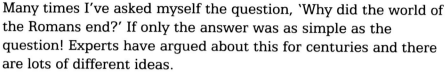

THE END OF ANCIENT ROME

The empire breaks up

This Roman fort, at Burgh Castle in Norfolk, England, was built as a defence against Saxon invaders. Many forts were built along the southern and eastern coast of Britain at this time, and experts call them Saxon Shore forts.

Many times I've asked myself the question, 'Why did the world of the Romans end?' If only the answer was as simple as the question! Experts have argued about this for centuries and there are lots of different ideas.

Rome's problems began towards the end of the third century AD. There was fighting between army generals over which of them should become the next emperor. Fewer men could be found to join the army, and without a strong army it was harder to defend the boundaries of the empire. Food prices rose due to problems with the economy, leading to high inflation. Do these problems seem familiar to you? Many problems we have today were faced by the Romans, too!

It was difficulties such as these that weakened the empire and led to its collapse. Groups of people from warlike tribes who lived outside the empire, whom the Romans regarded as uncivilized barbarians, began to penetrate deep behind Roman defences. Their attacks became more daring and in AD 410 Rome itself was captured by thousands of Visigoths who

Inside Santa Sophia. A Christian church converted to an Islamic mosque.
▼

The great church of Santa Sophia in Istanbul was built between the years AD 532 and 538. It was the most important Christian church in what was then Constantinople. It later became a mosque, dedicated to Islam. The towers (called minarets) were added in the 1500s.

Barbarian invasions

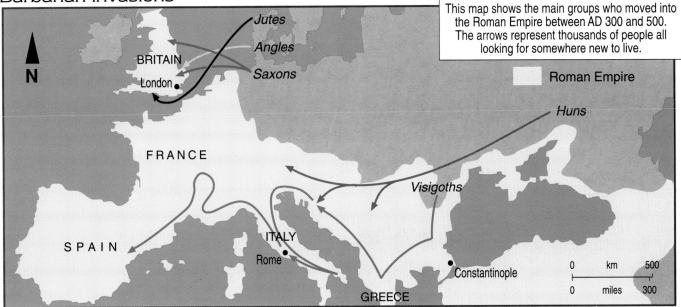

This map shows the main groups who moved into the Roman Empire between AD 300 and 500. The arrows represent thousands of people all looking for somewhere new to live.

☐ Roman Empire

Jutes
Angles
Saxons
BRITAIN
London
Huns
FRANCE
Visigoths
SPAIN
ITALY
Rome
Constantinople
GREECE

0 km 500
0 miles 300

were led by Alaric, their warrior king. The Visigoths had been forced out of their homeland in central Europe by invaders from Asia and Russia called Huns.

The province of Britain was threatened by groups of people from northern Europe called Saxons. So the Romans reinforced their defences with new forts built along the southern coast – but when the Roman army withdrew from Britain in the early 400s, Rome's most northerly province was left open to invasion. It was probably at this time that the wealthy Faustinus family buried their valuables – no doubt hoping to return for them when it was safe to do so. But they never did return (see page 32).

Fact File

A new Rome in the east

When Diocletian became emperor in AD 284 he set about making great changes. He divided the Roman Empire into two parts – a western and an eastern empire. He knew it was becoming harder to control a single massive empire and the split was his way of solving the problem. Each part had its own emperor – but quarrels broke out between them. Then, in AD 324, Emperor Constantine reunited the empire and for a time he was the sole ruler. Constantine made even greater changes than Diocletian. He was the emperor who accepted Christianity as the state religion (see page 40), and he also moved the capital from Rome to Byzantium, a city in the east. His plan was to build a new city that would be as great as Rome. The city he built became known as Constantinople (modern day Istanbul, a city in Turkey). While Rome grew to be the centre of Christianity in the west, Constantinople became the Christian centre in the east. It stayed this way for 1,000 years, until AD 1453 when Constantinople became an Islamic city.

The city of Ravenna in northeast Italy had many fine early Christian churches. Inside they were decorated with magnificent mosaics in the Byzantine style – a style developed in Constantinople and widely copied elsewhere.

Discovering the Romans

An excavation in progress at the Roman town of Verulamium (St Albans), in England.

There are many ways to discover the Romans. As an archaeologist I have excavated many Roman sites, always on the look out for something new that can give us fresh information. A few years ago no one would have thought that a remote Roman fort in northern Britain would yield wooden writing tablets – with messages that could still be read after 1,800 years (see page 33). When I saw these objects in the museum it was as if I was looking over the shoulder of the Roman who had just written on them – it was a really weird feeling!

But apart from finding everyday objects, how else are we discovering new facts about the Romans? One important way is to fly over farmers' fields at certain times of the year – usually when crops are growing. To the trained eye, patterns can be seen in the crops, showing the outlines of buried buildings or ancient field systems. Many Roman farms, lengths of road and even long-lost towns have been found this way, especially in Britain and France.

I know that when I was in Rome I'd wished for X-ray vision, and archaeologists working in Italy have actually devised a clever way of examining Etruscan tombs without digging into them (see page 10). They push a probe deep into the ground and into the tomb. A tiny video camera sends back a picture from inside the tomb. This way the archaeologists can decide if the tomb is worth excavating – before the 'clandestini' (tomb robbers) beat them to it!

Using a computer an archaeologist can draw a three-dimensional picture of a building. This computer image shows buildings inside a Roman fort. You can also see the wall around the fort, a gateway and a road. Some of these features can be seen in the photograph of Housesteads Fort on page 22.

Roman wall paintings are very fragile and have to be carefully restored. This picture of a woman looking into a mirror has been joined together from hundreds of broken pieces, and the missing areas have been cleverly painted in.

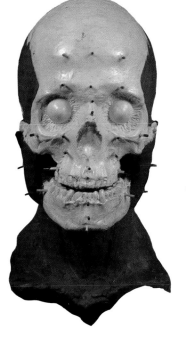

Reconstructing faces from skulls is a technique used by archaeologists and police – for very different reasons. Layers of special clay have been applied to this Roman skull by a medical artist. It is then possible to work out how the person may have looked when he was alive.

This photograph shows the outline of a Roman farmhouse buried in a field. It shows up like this because a crop will grow at a different rate if it is on top of a buried wall, where the soil is not as deep as elsewhere in the field. At ground level there may be no signs of the building at all. The straight lines that run down the picture are tracks from a modern vehicle, probably a tractor.

Fact File

Place names as evidence

You don't have to dig into the ground to look for signs of the Romans. Names of towns and villages can tell us if Romans used to live there. Look at this list of ten places in Britain that all have something in common. Can you see what it is?

Modern name	Meaning
1. Alcester	fort on the River Alne.
2. Chesterton	farm or village near a camp.
3. Chichester	Cissi's fort or town.
4. Colchester	fort on the River Colne.
5. Godmanchester	Godmund's fort or town.
6. Ilchester	fort on the River Yeo.
7. Kenchester	Cena's fort or town.
8. Portchester	fort by the harbour.
9. Towcester	fort on the River Tove.
10. Woodchester	fort in a wood.

In each case the name has either the word 'chester' or 'cester' in it. These words come from the Old English word 'ceaster' which means Roman camp or town. Other words, such as people's names (Cena, Cissi and Godmund, for example) were added to 'ceaster' to produce the name which is familiar to us. Place names can tell us if the Romans were in our own area. There are about 350 place names in Britain with Roman connections.

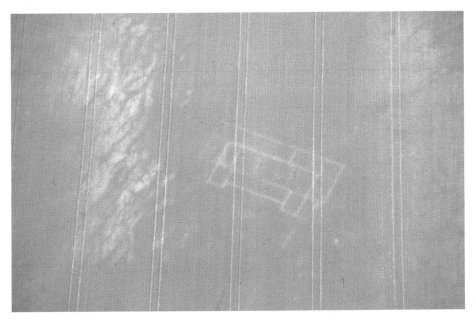

GLOSSARY

Amphitheatre – An open-air building used for gladiator and other shows.

Amphora – A type of storage pot for wine and oil.

Aqueduct – A narrow bridge to carry water across uneven land.

Augustus (63 BC – AD 14) – The first Roman emperor. He changed his name from Gaius Julius Caesar Octavianus to Augustus. Reigned 27 BC – AD 14.

Barbarians – Groups of people who lived outside the Roman world. The Romans regarded them as uncivilized and a danger to their rule.

Basilica – A large building at the centre of a town used by officials.

Byzantium – see **Constantinople.**

Julius Caesar (100–44 BC) – A powerful army general who was popular with the people but who was murdered by Roman senators.

Cameo – A carved semi-precious stone with two or more layers of colour.

Carroballista – A heavy-duty crossbow.

Carthage – The capital city of the Carthaginians in north Africa.

Catacombs – Underground passages in Rome used for burials and religious ceremonies.

Century – A unit of soldiers (80–100 men).

Circus Maximus – A racetrack in Rome.

Colosseum – An amphitheatre in Rome.

Constantine (AD 272–337) – The emperor who accepted Christianity. Reigned AD 312–337.

Constantinople – The city that replaced Rome as the capital. Present-day Istanbul, Turkey.

Consul – The most senior government official.

Diocletian (AD 245–313) – The emperor who divided the Roman Empire in two. Reigned AD 284–305.

Etruscans – A group of people who lived in Italy before the Romans.

Forum – A square at the centre of a Roman town used as a market-place.

Gaul – The area of present-day France and Belgium.

Gladiator – A professional fighter trained to fight to the death.

Hadrian's Wall – A stone wall in northern Britain built by Emperor Hadrian to mark a boundary of the Roman Empire.

Hannibal (247–183 BC) – Leader of the Carthaginians and enemy of Rome.

Herculaneum – City buried by lava when the volcano Vesuvius erupted in AD 79.

Insula – A block of buildings in a Roman town.

Latin – Language of the Romans.

Latium – Original homeland of the Romans.

Legion – A unit of soldiers (5,300 men).

Mosaic – A picture usually made from cubes of coloured stone.

Mount Vesuvius – An active volcano near the cities of Pompeii and Herculaneum.

Octavian – see **Augustus.**

Onager – A heavy-duty catapult.

Ostia – The port of Rome.

Pantheon – A temple building in Rome.

Patrician – A privileged, wealthy Roman.

Plebeian – An ordinary, poor Roman.

Pompeii – City buried by ash when the volcano Vesuvius erupted in AD 79.

Pompey (106–48 BC) – An army general who plotted against Julius Caesar.

Provincia (Province) – An area of the Roman Empire considered to belong to Rome.

Punic Wars – The wars between the Romans and the Carthaginians.

Romulus and Remus – The twins, who according to legend, were suckled by a wolf. Rome was named after Romulus.

Scipio (d.211 BC) – Roman general who defeated Hannibal.

Senator – One of about 600 politicians who governed Rome.

Stola – A gown worn by married women.

Strigil – A body scraper.

Stylus – A writing implement.

Tesserae – Cubes of coloured stone, glass or pottery used to make mosaic pictures.

Toga – The standard item of clothing for men.

Trajan (AD 52–117) – The emperor during whose reign the Roman Empire expanded to its greatest extent. Reigned AD 98–117.

Trajan's Column – A war memorial built in Rome to commemorate battle victories of Emperor Trajan.

Villa – A house in the countryside which was usually the centre of a large farm estate.

RAILWAYS IN AND ARO

C000291581

TAUNTON

SOMERSET & NORTH DEVON

Taunton. 5th August 1961. Taken from the footbridge ("forty steps") near Taunton West Junction, 43XX Class 2-6-0 No. **6378** is leaving on the 10.50am SO Wolverhampton-Minehead.
M.J.Fox

MICHAEL J. FOX

Bishops Lydeard, **22nd August 1964.** The 8.17am Taunton- Minehead waits at Bishops Lydeard behind train engine 61XX Class 2-6-2T No. **6148** and pilot NBL type 2 No. **D6336.** The fireman is receiving the first single line tablet on the branch which, since 1936, had been doubled from Norton Fitzwarren Junction as far as this first station.

M.J.Fox

RAILWAYS IN AND AROUND
TAUNTON
SOMERSET & NORTH DEVON

Introduction.

A visitor to Taunton station today would quickly sense that it had once been a much more complex railway centre. This becomes apparent through observing the four through tracks, the independent goods loop, and no less than ten platform faces, only three of which are still used by passengers. In earlier days the town was the focal point of a group of radiating branches and local services serving the surrounding area This was in addition to main-line services from both London, and from the north to the West Country, two separate streams of traffic which converged close to Taunton and were greatly augmented at summer weekends.

My own links with Taunton began in 1950 when my parents moved there from the Midlands and I attended a school beside the railway line. I continued to live in Taunton, excepting national service and university term, until 1961 when I still visited the town regularly until after the Beeching closures and the end of steam services in the district. My own recollections and photographic records have been amplified with the help of other contributors, to whom I am greatly indebted.

The time span which the book covers is essentially from Railway Nationalisation to Beeching Rationalisation, though readers will discover earlier scenes, and references to later events. The area covered within the book is bordered by Bridgwater, Castle Cary, Yeovil, Chard, Tiverton, Barnstaple and Minehead. This span seems to me to be appropriate on several counts:

— *It fits in well with my own photographic collection,and the size of book desired by the publisher.*
— *It reflects the WR operations centred on Taunton without introducing independent SR and S&DJR activities.*

Cogload Junction, 12th June 1958. 4073 Class 4-6-0 No. **7029** *Clun Castle* on the flyover crossing the direct London (Via Westbury) lines with the 11.55am Manchester-Plymouth train. *R.J.Sellick*

— *Its borders include what are now, sadly, the nearest surviving BR stations in each direction to which one can travel direct from Taunton, namely Bridgwater, Castle Cary, and Tiverton Parkway, together with two other surviving stations at Yeovil Pen Mill and Barnstaple.*

My decision to avoid any consideration of, for example, the SR Salisbury-Exeter main line or the S&DJR where they skirt my selected area is in no way due to GWR bias. On the contrary, my impressionable years were lived within walking distance of an LMS Western Division shed, and I have never been able to accept Swindon products without domes as being complete engines. Rather, the omissions are because I feel that these neighbouring lines deserve fuller coverage themselves. For the present, let us bask in the memory of sunny summer Saturdays around Tarn'n.

Acknowledgements.

One of the pleasures of producing a book like this is the opportunity to get to know people who, at the outset, were often complete strangers. In the present case I must thank fellow photographers Hugh Ballantyne, Peter Gray, Ron Lumber, Dick Riley, Wilf Underhay, S.J.Dickson, P.J.Kelley and Roger Venning for searching out negatives or prints which might be useful to me, and identifying the subject matter. My particular thanks go to John Alves both for photographs and for his recollections of the GWR at Taunton, which reach back beyond my birth date. Acknowledgement is also due to Lens of Sutton, for permission to reproduce prints supplied from negatives held in their collections. Finally my gratitude to another Fox, Gregory who is not only the publisher but also an essential collaborator in creating this book. *M.J.Fox*

Historical background

Taunton is the county town of Somerset, situated towards the western edge of the county. From north or east Taunton is approached across the low-lying Somerset Levels, but south and west the land is more hilly, the Vale of Taunton Deane being almost encircled by the Blackdown, Quantock and Brendon hills.

Before the arrival of the railway Taunton was served by a network of turnpike roads, just as now it is closely skirted by the M5 motorway. It was also for a time the focus of a group of canals, now largely forgotten; the Bridgwater & Taunton, Grand Western, and Chard Canals.

After the Great Western Railway had completed its line from Paddington to Bristol, the next stage in extending railways into the West Country was the Bristol & Exeter Railway. Complementing the Great Western Railway, with which it was closely associated, like the GWR it was built to Broad Gauge. This is the line which put Taunton and the surrounding district on the railway map. Opened to Exeter in 1844, it was taken over by the GWR in 1876. The gauge difference helped to keep the B&E and its feeders separate from the infiltration of standard-gauge (the GWR would have said narrow-gauge) rivals, and can be seen as one of the reasons for the area described remaining exclusively "Western" territory.

The B&E route passed within a few miles of Tiverton but did not serve the town directly; consequently in 1848 a short branch was built from Tiverton Junction station (previously Tiverton Road) at the village of Willand.

Although Taunton is the centre of the area we are examining, it was not significantly the largest town. Bridgwater and Yeovil were and are of comparable size, and both had (and still retain) more industrial activity than Taunton. Bridgwater had its docks, and brick and tile works; Yeovil a traditional lace and glove making industry. In this century more modern industries developed, resulting in such sites as the British Cellophane factory at Bridgwater and the Westland aircraft works at Yeovil. Taunton,

as County Town and centre of a rich farming area was more concerned with agriculture and local administration. The key witnesses of Taunton's strategic contribution to the railway's revenues, apart from the varied branch lines feeding into it, was the large goods warehouse and the nearby cattle market.

The B&E route passed through Bridgwater some 11 miles the Bristol side of Taunton, but not Yeovil in South Somerset. In consequence the next line to be built in our chosen area, forming the first of the branches radiating from Taunton, was one linking both Taunton and Bridgwater with Yeovil. This was opened in 1853 from Durston on the B&E.

The Taunton-Yeovil line was followed during the 1860s by two more branches: The first was the "West Somerset Railway" to Watchet, a small port on the Bristol Channel. It left the main line at Norton Fitzwarren, the first station west of Taunton, and skirted the western side of the Quantocks. It was opened in 1862. The second of these lines went south from Creech Junction just east of Taunton, to the town of Chard, and was opened in 1866. Chard was also served by a "narrow" gauge branch from Chard Junction on the LSWR to Chard Town. After the GWR's broad gauge lines were converted to standard gauge (the Chard branch was one of the very last to be regauged) the two lines to Chard were linked and worked throughout from Taunton to Chard Junction by the GWR.

The 1870s found three further lines built. In 1873 the Devon and Somerset Railway was opened to Barnstaple; like the West Somerset Railway it left the main line at Norton Fitzwarren but threaded the southern edges of the Brendons and Exmoor. The following year, 1874, an extension to the WSR was opened from Watchet to Minehead. The third line completed during the 1870s was a locally promoted line, the Culm Valley Light Railway from Tiverton Junction to Hemyock, completed in 1876.

During the next decade Tiverton was linked to the Devon and Somerset line by the Tiverton and North Devon line, opened

Taunton, 20th September 1947. Platform 7, just pulling into the station from the carriage sidings is No. **2946** *Langford Court* with a Taunton - Bristol stopping train. It should be noted that when the bay platform 9 (to the right of the locomotive) was being used by a Taunton - Yeovil branch train, as in this case, then the Taunton - Bristol stoppers used platform 7.

R.Venning

to Morebath Junction on the D&S in 1884. Only a year later Tiverton was linked more directly to Exeter via the Exe Valley line to Stoke Canon on the B&E main line. Operationally these two lines were effectively part of the same route, trains working through from Exeter to terminate at Dulverton on the D&S. In 1887 a connection was created from the D&S, just short of its Victoria Road terminus in Barnstaple, to the LSWR line at Barnstaple Junction.

This completes the account of construction up until the time that the broad gauge was eliminated from the main line in 1892. By this time all the branches mentioned had been converted to standard gauge, if they had previously been broad or mixed gauge.

The final piece in our jigsaw is a significant one. While trains to the west travelled via Bristol the rumour that GWR stood for Great Way Round could seem well-founded. The new direct route from Paddington via Westbury was created by means of a cut off line from Castle Cary on the Wilts, Somerset and Weymouth to a junction (Curry Rivell Junction) on the Taunton-Yeovil line just outside the little town of Langport. The new line was opened in 1906. The existing junction at Durston was bypassed by another much shorter stretch of new line, from Athelney to Cogload near Creech St. Michael. Since the original single line was not closed,

stopping trains could use either the old or the new route to and from Athelney.

The congestion caused by the convergence of the two routes west of Cogload Junction was relieved during the 1930s, by creating a flying junction at Cogload, and progressively extending a quadruple-track main line through Taunton station, and then as far as Norton Fitzwarren Junction. In addition Halts were opened on several of the lines radiating from Taunton to counter bus competition, most of them in the late 1920s. Later in the 1930s subsidised works were put in hand to improve the capacity of the Minehead and Barnstaple branches.

The rest of the story in the present century is contraction of the network during the 1960s, together with closure of all the smaller main-line stations, followed by resignalling and track simplification in the late 1980s.

The route between Cogload Junction and Norton Fitzwarren was much the most intensively operated in the area and I hope that the detailed map of these four track sections will help to explain how the traffic flows were segregated or combined, and how the various platforms of Taunton station coped with specific services during the period covered by the photographs, i.e. from the late thirties to the early sixties.

Taunton West, August 1947. Manchester - Penzance express hauled by No. **6022** *King Henry IV* passing the "Avimo" instrument factory soon after leaving Taunton station.   *R. Venning*

Taunton station

Taunton, 11th August 1962. View from the No. 3 Bay platform at the west end of Taunton Station with Class 43XX 2-6-0 No. **4326** awaiting departure with a Barnstaple train. "Hall" Class No. **4917** *Crosswood Hall* approaches the station with the 10.18am Newton Abbot - Bradford working, and will shortly pass West Station signal box. ***P.W.Gray***

Like many early major stations built under Brunel's influence, Taunton was originally single-sided. That is to say, facilities for both Up and Down trains were located on the south (Down) side of the line, with all of the conflicting movements this entailed. The Down side was chosen as being nearest to the town, though the town centre was still some mile away from the station. Some of the original range of buildings still survive, though the single-sided arrangement only lasted until 1868 when it was replaced by a station of orthodox layout with all-over roof. As the branches were opened and traffic increased it was not long before congestion again became severe.

During 1895/1896 the platforms were extended and bays were added, and a separate goods loop avoiding the station was constructed. Taunton station was finally extended yet again during 1930-32, during which four main-line through platforms were created. a new low level entrance on the Up side, and a subway connecting platforms and entrances. At the same time the overall roof and footbridge were removed. This is the state of Taunton station depicted in all of the photographs of Taunton included in this book. The Up entrance is the one in use today, with the more recent addition of a "travel centre"; the Down side entrance was closed when the station's services were reduced, but entry from that side was re-established more recently when Taunton became an open station.

One intriguing feature which persisted until well into BR days, associated with the two entrances, was the existence of two separate booking offices with segregated stocks of tickets. At the Down side office tickets were only available for destinations in the Down direction, and vice-versa for the Up office. If you presented yourself at the wrong office relative to your destination you were supplied with a free platform ticket to pass through the subway to the other side.

The track layout diagram (see pages 8/9) will show the configuration of the station better than a verbal description, but I will explain the use of each platform. Platform 1 was the Down Relief, platform 5 Down Main, platform 6 Up Main, and platform 7 Up Relief. Main line trains stopping at Taunton normally used the relief platforms; the main platforms were also used when two trains travelling in the same direction had to be handled simultaneously, but otherwise only non-stop trains were routed through the main platforms. In consequence, the island platform between the Up and Down Mains had more limited passenger facilities, e.g. no refreshment room. In addition, stopping trains might use the through roads, but branch trains and main-line trains starting or terminating at Taunton could also make use of the bays.

Trains to or from Minehead and Barnstaple tended to arrive or depart in quick succession, since they normally connected with the same main line train. So bays 3 and 4 were typically used to hold Down trains to Minehead and Barnstaple, waiting side by side. Such an occasion is captured in one of the photographs. A stopping train to Exeter might also leave from one of these bays, though these were not frequent and some originated at Bristol. Bay 8 was used for Minehead or Barnstaple arrivals, Bay 9 for departures to Yeovil, Castle Cary, or Bristol. Bay 2 was used by the Chard trains, both arrivals and departures being accommodated. Nevertheless a Chard departure from platform 2 had great scope for delaying other trains, since it had to cross Down Relief, Down Main and Up Main in order to gain the Down Relief, and within about two miles reversed the procedure at Creech Junction!

After closure of the branches and reduction in freight services, Taunton's facilities have shrunk again. Nowadays the main line is quadruple only through the station itself. The Up and Down Main platforms are intact but not used by passengers; the buildings and canopy are removed and entrance from the subway closed. In fact the only platforms still in use are the former 1, 7 and 9, now renumbered 1, 2 and 3.

Through Train Services.

The most smartly timed main line services using Taunton in the post-nationalisation steam era were, in general, the trains to and from Paddington via Westbury. This is true even though the most prestigious trains such as the Cornish Riviera Express (Paddington-Penzance) and the Torbay Express (Paddington-Kingswear) did not stop at Taunton. There was also a Paddington-Bristol-Taunton service but although these often ran as expresses to Bristol, they would change engines at Bristol and then run semi-fast to Taunton serving Yatton, Weston, Highbridge and Bridgwater.

Regarding services to the north it is easy to forget how nationalisation, electrification and Intercity 125s have changed the pattern since steam days. Whereas nowadays most trains are routed via Birmingham, in the 1950s the traffic patterns still followed pre-nationalisation logic. For the GWR the desirable route for a train from Plymouth to Manchester was via the Severn Tunnel, Shrewsbury and Hereford joint line, and Crewe. This way the LMS's share of the journey was only the miles north of Shrewsbury. With one exception a passenger from Taunton to Yorkshire or Tyneside via the Midland Bristol-Birmingham line would have had to change at Bristol. That exception was the Paignton-Bradford Devonian express.

The final named train to be mentioned is the Cornishman, which was a Wolverhampton Low Level-Penzance train. Being a service which had originated in GWR days, it avoided using the LMR Birmingham-Bristol line until Cheltenham, through travelling from the WR Snow Hill station, by way of Stratford-on-Avon and Honeybourne.

Taunton, 7th April 1962. 6959 Class (Modified Hall) 4-6-0 No. **7916** *Mobberley Hall* and an Up goods train pass under Staplegrove Road bridge and pass Taunton West Junction Box. *M.J.Fox*

Local train services.

Stopping trains between Bristol and Exeter have already been mentioned. There was one further main-line stopping service, to Castle Cary; which utilised push-pull auto-trains until about 1960. Branch trains operated to Minehead, Barnstaple (or Ilfracombe), Chard and Yeovil. On summer Saturdays there were through trains to Minehead and Ilfracombe from such places as Manchester, Cardiff and Wolverhampton, the trains splitting at Taunton. There were also through trains on summer Saturdays between Paddington and Minehead. On weekdays a typical formation for most of these branch trains at Taunton was a "B set", which comprised a pair of matching brake-composite compartment coaches, each including just one first-class compartment, close-coupled at the inner ends. As needed, e.g. in the summer, and particularly at weekends, the "B set" would be strengthened by one or even two corridor coaches. Redundant slip coaches were popular for this purpose, since the lack of through corridor connections was no disadvantage.

The trains serving Tiverton were normally push-pull with auto-fitted trailers. The Culm Valley line, due to its extremely tight curvature was a special case, in respect of both locomotives and carriages, which will be described at the appropriate section of the book.

Goods services.

Main line services were light compared to many trunk routes, mainly because of the limited amount of mineral traffic traversing this predominantly pastoral area. Originating traffic was largely agricultural and, especially, perishable fruit and vegetables. Thus a large proportion of trains were of fitted or semi-fitted nature. Parcels and milk traffic was also significant. Because of the intensive passenger traffic, goods trains on summer Saturdays were virtually absent during daylight hours.

Branch goods traffic was also limited in intensity; each branch had typically one goods train a day, except for the Taunton-Barnstaple line which was busier, handling through traffic for North Devon. The Culm Valley branch's traffic was handled by means of a mixed train, and any passenger train was likely to transport one or a few milk tankers.

Main-line motive power.

These notes are a summary of the practices observed during the post-nationalisation steam period. The Paddington-West of England line was a "double-red" restriction line, and so permitted for all classes including Kings. Nearly all direct Paddington expresses would be King or Castle hauled. Of the named trains the Cornish Riviera was a King.............. ***Continued on page 10***

Taunton c 1962. A panoramic view along the northerly face of the island platform. **No 5** is to the left and **No 6** to the right. The up train faces platform 7 over to the right. Looking from the east end of the station looking towards Norton Fitzwarren   **G. H. Platt**

Taunton
Station Layout c.1953

Taunton, 7th April 1962. 4073 Class 4-6-0 No. **5023** *Brecon Castle* passes Taunton West Junction on an Up freight; whilst 43XX Class 2-6-0 No. **7326** stands with a two coach train, probably the empty stock of an arrival from Barnstaple. *M.J.Fox*

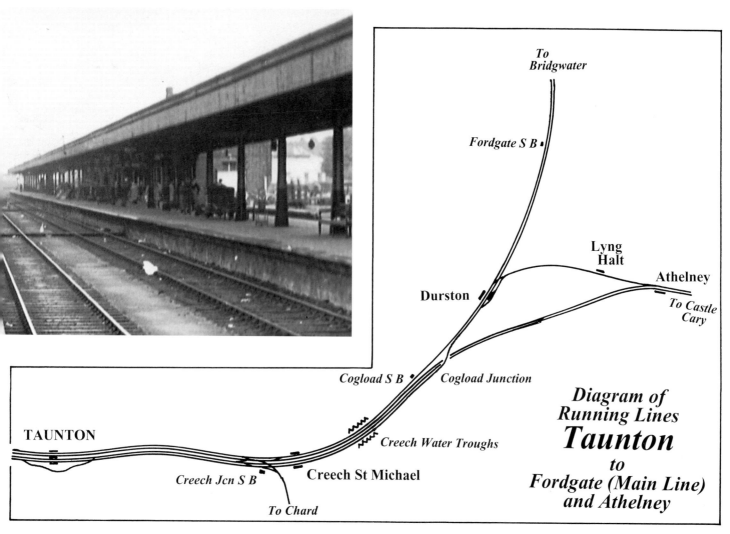

Diagram of Running Lines **Taunton** *to* **Fordgate (Main Line) and Athelney**

To Bridgwater

Fordgate S B

Lyng Halt

Athelney

To Castle Cary

Durston

Cogload S B — Cogload Junction

Creech Water Troughs

TAUNTON

Creech Jcn S B — Creech St Michael

To Chard

working as far as Plymouth but the lighter Torbay Express to and from Paignton was handled by a selected Newton Abbot Castle.

Some of the Paddington-Bristol expresses continued semi-fast to Taunton, after changing engines at Bristol. Stopping trains between Bristol and Exeter might employ Stars or Saints during the earlier 1950s, but Castles or Halls were normal on the long-distance trains via Bristol. The Cornishman (Penzance-Wolverhampton) and Devonian (Paignton-Bradford) were both Castle-hauled south of Bristol where they changed engines. Counties and Britannia's were less common, and Manors were rare except on summer Saturdays, which also brought the 47XX express freight 2-8-0s one regular passenger diagram.

The depots providing the motive power for most of these workings were Old Oak Common, Newton Abbot, Laira and Bristol (Bath Road). Through goods traffic was hauled by 28XX 2-8-0s, 43XX 2-6-0s, Granges, Halls (especially as dieselisation encroached on their passenger workings) and sometimes WD or Stanier 8F 2-8-0s.

Taunton shed.

Taunton shed was GWR code TN, later BR code 83B under Newton Abbot district. It had an allocation of between 50 and 60 engines, mainly for fairly local needs. The actual shed building was a single roundhouse of standard design for the late Dean period, the building having been constructed in 1896. There was an adjacent repair shop, which unlike the rest of the shed buildings still stands, and typical GWR coaling stage with a ramp leading up to the wagon unloading point. The location of the shed was on the west side of Station Road, sandwiched between the station's platform 3 and the goods loop. The shed was closed in 1964. The allocation for a date during 1939 is given, courtesy of

Taunton, 10th August 1962. Taken from the footbridge ("forty steps") near Taunton West Junction, Western Diesel-Hydraulic No. **D1O06** Western Stalwart passes on the Down Cornish Riviera Express. In the distance are the station (behind the signal gantry) and loco shed. The goods loop is to the right of the long line of coaches.   *M.J.Fox*

John Alves, and developments after Nationalisation are summarised here.

After 1948 Taunton's stud of tender engines included a half-dozen or so Halls and Granges, mainly for the Paddington-Bristol-Taunton trains, and a number of 43XX 2-6-0s which were the mainstay of the Barnstaple line as well as having mainline duties. Other tender engines included 2251 class 0-6-0s which had replaced the Dean Goods 0-6-0 and were in turn displaced from the district later in the 1950s by additional Large Prairie 2-6-2Ts. Around 1960 Taunton briefly acquired its only pure height engines in the shape of two 28XX 2-8-0s to work sulphuric acid trains between Merseyside and the British Cellophane plant at Bridgwater. Last but by no means least, Taunton usually had one Castle allocated, on standby to cover for mainline express failures. During much of the fifties this was 5003 Lulworth Castle, followed by 5061 Earl of Birkenhead.

Amongst tank engine classes, Taunton had a large allocation of 45XX Small Prairie 2-6-2Ts, mostly of the 4575 series with additional water capacity. These did a great deal of branch line work, especially to Minehead and Yeovil. A few Large Prairie 2-6-2T of class 51XX were allocated, mainly for Wellington banking duties, main-line stopping trains and local goods. When Taunton's 2251 class 0-6-0s had been transferred away, more Large Prairies arrived and took over many Minehead workings The new arrivals included class 61XX engines from the London area, where they had been displaced by DMUs.

The pannier tanks were mainly class 57XX for shunting, local freight and branch passenger work, auto-fitted Class 54XX for the Castle Cary auto-trains which Taunton shared with Westbury shed, and also a solitary 74XX. However much the most interesting shunting engines were the varied stud subshedded at Bridgwater for the docks branch. At different times from 1950 these included ancient Wolverhampton-built 2021 class 0-6-0PTs, their BR-built 16XX class replacements, a 1361 class 0-6-0ST, a 1366 class 0-6-0PT, Cardiff Railway 0-4-0ST 1338 and my favourite of all these, ex-Burry Port and Gwendraeth Valley Railway 0-6-0ST 2194 Kidwelly.

Taunton concrete works had a Simplex petrol shunter, for its departmental shunting needs.

0-6-0	Class 2251 (Collett)	2261, 2266, 2267, 2268, 2275.
	Class 2301 (Dean)	2410, 2418, 2472, 2527, 2537, 2578.
4-4-0	Class 3300 (Bulldog)	3361
		3443 Chaffinch
		3444 Cormorant
2-6-2T	Class 51XX	4117, 5148, 5172.
	Class 4575	4581, 5501, 5502, 5503, 5504, 5521, 5522, 5525, 5537, 5542, 5569, 557 2708
0-6-0PT	Class 655	
	Class 1701	1760, 1897, 1899.
	Class 2021	2050, 2127.
	Class 57XX	9750, 9757.
	Class 74XX	7421.
2-4-0T	Class 455 (Metro)	3582, 3590.
0-4-2T	Class 58XX	5812

TOTAL : 56

Taunton Shed, 11th July 1946. 2251 Class No. **2266** standing over the inspection pit at the entrance to Taunton roundhouse. *J.Alves*

The allocation presented below is reproduced through the courtesy of John Alves.

LOCOMOTIVES ALLOCATED TO TAUNTON DEPOT
At 30th April 1939

4-6-0	Class 4073(Castle)	5077 Eastnor Castle
	Class 40XX (Star)	4026 Japanese Monarch
		4054 Princess Charlotte
		4056 Princess Margaret
	Class 49XX(Hall)	4954 Plaish Hall
		5985 Knolton Hall
2-6-0	Class 43XX	6323, 6354, 6363, 6364, 6372, 6383, 6398, 7314.

Taunton, 9th July 1946. 1701 Class 0-6-0PT No. **1760** standing near coaling stage after returning on the Dulverton pick up goods. *J.Alves*

Taunton, 11th July 1946. Chargehand Fred Rowlands poses with two of his lady cleaners, on the running plate of No. **4908** *Broom Hall.* *J.Alves*

Bridgwater-Taunton

The Bristol and Exeter Railway was extended from Bridgwater to Taunton in 1842, converted from broad to mixed gauge in 1875, and to standard gauge in 1892. Passing over the Somerset levels it was easily graded, and initially with no engineering features of note except Somerset Bridge over the River Parrett, a shallow masonry arch like Brunel's similar bridge over the Thames at Maidenhead. In contrast to the Maidenhead bridge, which did not collapse as contemporary opinion thought it would, Somerset Bridge did give trouble. The present bridge is a steel lattice girder replacement.

The intermediate station of Durston originated as the junction for Yeovil when that line was built. The station had three platforms; Up and Down Main, plus a third platform for trains arriving off the branch. There was also an unusual signal box, of 'L' plan with one face parallel to the platforms and the other at right-angles.

At Cogload Junction, named after a nearby farm, the Down B&E line now passes over the direct Paddington lines by means of a flyover, built in 1930, similar to the better-known one on the SR at Battledown where the Bournemouth and Salisbury lines diverge. Nearby were Creech (or Cogload) water troughs, conveniently fed from the adjacent Bridgwater and Taunton Canal, which the GWR had acquired many years previously. After quadrupling of the main line between Cogload and Taunton, there was no physical connection between Paddington and Bristol lines until nearer Taunton where they became the Main and Relief respectively.

After quadrupling, Creech St. Michael Halt (opened 1928) had platforms only on the Bristol lines, and a little way west of the halt the Chard line joined the main line at Creech Junction. Quadrupling of the main line involved reconstruction of Taunton station. and a goods avoiding line had also been built earlier, in 1896, to provide some relief to the very cramped station. This left the passenger lines at Taunton East Junction, and beside the loop

Bridgwater General, 25th September 1958. A view of the station looking north towards Bristol, with "Castle" 4-6-0 No. **5079** *Lysander* passing on the Bradford-Paignton "Devonian" Train.   *J.Sellick*

was built a new and very large goods shed.

On the opposite side of the line, at the eastern approach to the passenger station, was the Civil Engineer's depot where prefabricated concrete structures were manufactured.

The stations at Creech St. Michael and Durston were closed in 1964, when the Taunton-Yeovil service was withdrawn.

Bridgwater General, c.1950's. This undated photograph, taken in BR days, is looking south towards Taunton. Since the station nameboard reads simply "Bridgwater", the view probably dates from after the closure of the S&DJR Bridgwater North station in 1951.   *Lens of Sutton*

BRIDGWATER DOCKS BRANCH

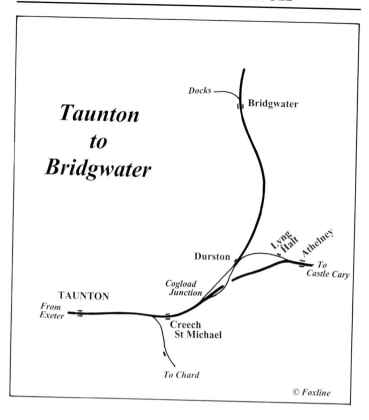

Bridgwater Docks, 5th August 1950. This Motor-Rail "Simplex" petrol shunter No. **15** was the first supplied to the GWR, and one of the varied collection of small engines which found use at Bridgwater because of weight restrictions and curvature on the docks branch. *P.W.Gray*

Bridgwater Docks, 7th July 1959. Ex-Cardiff Railway 0-4-0ST No. **1338,** built by Kitson, was another Bridgwater Docks shunter for a number of years. It is seen here on the quayside beside the River Parrett.
R.C.Riley

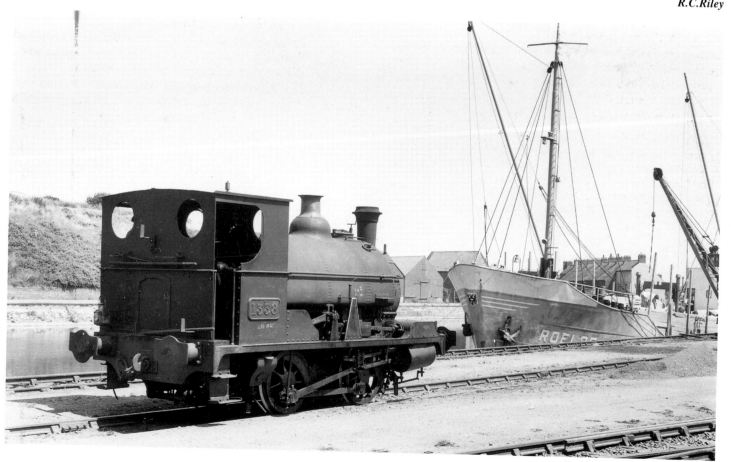

Durston, 22nd June 1963. 28XX Class 2-8-0 No. **2822** is approaching Durston with a Down goods train from Bristol direction. Taunton shed rarely had any mineral engines allocated to it, but at that time **2822** and **2882** were amongst its allocation, primarily in order to work chemical traffic for British Cellophane Ltd's plant at Bridgwater.

M.J.Fox

Durston, 23rd June 1962. 45XX Class 2-6-2T No. **4507** starting out of the Up Main platform with the 9.10am Taunton-Yeovil. The signal box was of an unusual "L" shaped plan; another angle is seen in the photograph of **82044** in the branch platform.

W.L.Underhay

Durston, 16th May 1965. Standard 3MT 2-6-2T No. **82044** draws into the branch platform with the 11.21am Yeovil Pen Mill-Taunton Train.

M.J.Fox

Situted some six miles and ten minutes from Taunton, **Durston** enjoyed services on both the main Bristol/West of England line and the branch from Yeovil. In the winter 1959/60 timetable, there were morning and afternoon trains direct or with through carriages to and from Paddington, the remainder operating on a basic Bristol/Taunton service. During the week, there were some nine main line trains each way; extra early afternoon workings, one each way, operated on Saturdays. The branch service however comprised three eastbound workings during the week and six in the westerly direction towards Taunton. Extra trains one in each direction, were provided on Saturdays. Durston closed its doors to passengers on 5th October 1964, along with Creech St.Michael.

Durston, 16th August 1961. 49XX Class 4-6-0 No. **5921** *Bingley Hall* restarting the 9.00am Bristol-Taunton stopping train. *M.J.Fox*

(Above) **Durston, 14th August 1963.** 57XX Class 0-6-0PT No. **9670** passing Durston with an Up pick-up goods train. The platform face serving the single line branch to Athelney can be seen to the left of the main line platforms. *M.J.Fox*

Durston, 17th August 1961. 57XX Class 0-6-0PT No. **4612** leaving on the 10.18am Castle Cary-Taunton stopper. The 8 minute journey, or perhaps ramble would be more appropriate, called en route at no less than ten intermediate stations in the 28 miles travelled. Alford Halt, Keinton Mandeville, Charlton Mackrell, Somerton, Long Sutton & Pitney, Langport East, Athelney, Lyng Halt and Creech St.Michael all provided stopping places in addition to Durston. *M.J.Fox*

Cogload Junction, 20th August 1961. 6959 Class (Modified Hall) 4-6-0 No. **7924** *Thornycroft Hall* using the Bristol line with a Taunton-Weymouth excursion, routed over the single line from Durston, and advertised to pick up at Creech St. Michael, Durston and Lyng Halt. At Cogload the line runs close to the Bridgwater & Taunton Canal (which provided the water for Cogload troughs); the canal is visible beside the tail of the train. *M.J.Fox*

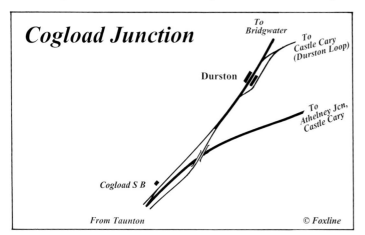

Cogload Junction.

The first thing to notice from the detail map of this location is that there was no physical junction at Cogload; through Creech St.Michael the Bristol lines flanked the direct lines, and only approaching Taunton station were trains transferred from one to the other. From this point, through Taunton station and on to Norton Fitzwarren, the inner lines became the Main and the outer ones the Relief. The creation of this flyover was the first stage of the improvement of track capacity through Taunton initiated in the 1930s.

Cogload Junction, c.1946. An unidentified Bulldog 4-4-0 crosses the flyover with a Yeovil-Taunton train via Durston. *J.Alves*

Cogload Junction, 23rd June 1962. Trains to and from Bristol pass during the steam/diesel-hydraulic transition of the Western Region. The Up train is headed by Warship No. **D860** *Victorious*, and the Down train by an unidentified Hymek.   *W. L.Underhay*

Cogload (Creech) water troughs, 14th May 1950. The troughs were located on the four-track section of line between Cogload Junction and Creech St.Michael, fed from the adjacent Bridgwater and Taunton Canal. In this view "Star" 4-6-0 No. **4033** *Queen Victoria* is passing on a Down express from the Bristol direction.   *R.J.Sellick*

Creech St. Michael Halt, 11th August 1961. 4575 Class 2-6-2T No. **5571** passes non-stop on the 9.45am Taunton-Yeovil, first stop Athelney. It will be clear why unless travelling via Durston, Yeovil and Castle Cary locals were unable to pick up at Creech. The leading vehicle in this train is a former slip coach; several were transferred to Taunton to strengthen local sets after slip workings on the main line ended. The group of large buildings in the distance was Creech paper mill, situated in the angle of the main line and Chard branch at Creech Junction.

M.J.Fox

Taunton, 20th July 1963. Type 3 Hymek Diesel-Hydraulic No. **D7065** leaving platform 7 with the 2.20pm SO Minehead-Paddington. *M.J.Fox*

G.W.R.

TAUNTON

(Above) Taunton, 5th August 1961. 47XX Class 2-8-0 No. **4701** passing Taunton non-stop on the Down Main with the 1.20pm SO Paddington-Kingswear. The nine engines of this class were intended for working heavy fitted freights, but use on a passenger train such as this was common on summer Saturdays.　　　*M.J.Fox*

Taunton Engineer's Depot, 23rd April 1955. A Motor-Rail Simplex petrol shunter No. **24** outside the perimeter wall of the depot. The loco had its own small corrugated iron shed and could be operated by staff who were not qualified to drive outside the depot. The concrete depot was established in Taunton towards the end of the last century but it was perhaps known more for the many standard items which became familiar in the 1930's & 40's as the use of concrete increased. Following the rationalisation of British Railway Workshops in the 1960's, the Western Region retained the facility here at the expense of other depots. Latterly it worked closely with the London Midland depot at Newton Heath Manchester to control the range of concrete products.　　　*M.J.Fox*

Taunton, 13th June 1964. SR Class U 2-6-0 No. **31802** of Yeovil SR (72C) shed waiting departure from platform 6, the Up Main, on the 4.25pm to Yeovil Pen Mill. This was the last day of Taunton -Yeovil services.

P.W.Gray

Taunton, 14th March 1964. SR Class U 2-6-0 No. **31792** of Yeovil SR (72C) shed awaiting departure from platform 7 (Up relief) with the 9.45am to Yeovil Pen Mill, and being overtaken by Class 4073 4-6-0 No. **7020** *Gloucester Castle,* passing through platform 6 (Up Main) on a fitted van train.

P.W.Gray

Taunton, c.1938. 2301 Class (Dean Goods) 0-6-0 No. **2472** standing at platform 7 with the through coaches from Minehead of an express to Paddington. Note the locomotive's branch train identification target: "M" for Minehead. In the years to come, less venerable motive power would carry out this function, although the chocolate and cream liveried coaching stock would remain familiar for the next two decades. Into the 1960's there were still two through trains between Minehead and Paddington on summer Saturdays. The opening in 1962 of Butlins at Minehead should have, one would think, ensured a longer life for the branch. *J.Alves*

Taunton, 5th July 1946. 10XX Class 4-6-0 No. **1018** *County of Leicester,* standing in platform 7 on the ex 9.05am Kingswear-Bradford. With something like a quarter of the journey to West Yorkshire behind them, passengers on this cross country train are still faced with another six hours of travel. This working followed the route and approximate times of the 'Devonian' which had been suspended during the war years. However, a few months after this photograph was taken, the 'Devonian' was reinstated albeit with an increased journey time. *J.Alves*

Taunton, 28th April 1938. Class 58XX 0-4-2T No. **5812,** as station pilot, standing in the Chard Bay (platform 2). Taunton acquired this engine after it ceased to be used on the Hemyock Branch. The service to Chard at its best, rarely seem to exceed the advertised seven or eight return workings, in fact only one, the 6.45pm ex Taunton, ran to the same schedules over the last thirty years of timetabling. In the last year of operation, 1962, there were five trains each way during the week taking an average 40 minutes for the 15 mile journey. The stations at Thornfalcon, Hatch, Ilton Halt, Iliminster, Donyatt Halt and Chard Central all closed on the 10th September 1962. *J.Alves*

Durston-Yeovil Pen Mill

The branch was opened in 1853. Although the passenger service was between Taunton and Yeovil (and moreover some trains used the main line between Cogload Junction and Athelney, so avoiding Durston) the GWR treated the branch as commencing at Durston. One reason for this was that the mixed gauge was provided in 1867 from the Wilts, Somerset & Weymouth line at Yeovil Pen Mill to Bridgwater and thence Highbridge (involving reversal at Durston) rather than to Taunton which remained solely broad gauge until 1875. This was influenced by a desire to offer a standard-gauge goods service from Bristol to English Channels to compete with that of the Somerset & Dorset Railway, and block the latter's parliamentary bill for a branch to Bridgwater. The original Yeovil terminus had been at Hendford but, after the arrival of the Salisbury and Yeovil Railway in an end-on junction in 1860, a further connection was made from the latter's Yeovil Town station to Yeovil Pen Mill, on the Wilts, Somerset and Weymouth. Yeovil Town was much more convenient for the town centre than Pen

Mill. Thus, throughout the period illustrated, there was a shuttle service to Yeovil Town from Yeovil Junction on the SR Salisbury-Exeter main line (the Salisbury & Yeovil was taken over by the LSWR and extended to Exeter), and also between Pen Mill and Yeovil Town on Sundays, and after withdrawal of the Taunton trains. Some SR line stopping trains serving Salisbury or Exeter started or terminated at Yeovil Town.

Yeovil had two loco depots, the LSWR/SR one being located adjacent to Yeovil Town station, and the GWR one at Pen Mill. The SR shed had BR code 72C under Exmouth Junction, and WR 82E under Bristol Bath Road. However, regional boundary changes caused the GWR shed to be transferred to the Southern Region before its closure, becoming 71H under Eastleigh district. Resulting changes in loco workings include the occasional use of 72C Class U 2-6-0s on Yeovil-Taunton trains in the last year or so before closure of the line, and GWR 54XX and 64XX 0-6-0PTs and trailers succeeding M7 0-4-4Ts on the Yeovil Junction- Yeovil Town push and pull train.

Another result of regional boundary changes was that some of the intermediate stations were resignalled with SR upper quadrant signals during the last years of the branch's life.

Perhaps the most interesting feature of the branch was the way, mentioned earlier, that the services had to adapt to the creation of the cut-off line via Westbury. The bypassed section of the branch (between Athelney and Durston) was kept open. Some Yeovil trains continued to run via the old route, maintaining a service to Creech, Durston and Lyng Halt, whilst others sprinted non-stop on the main line between Taunton and Athelney. After the 1930 quadrupling was implemented, Creech St. Michael Halt (opened 1928) had platforms on the Bristol lines only.

Loco diagrams for the Taunton-Yeovil line were shared by Taunton and Yeovil Pen Mill, both sheds normally using Small Prairie tanks until near the end, when BR Class 3 2-6-2T's became common.

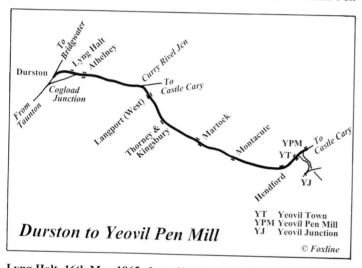

Durston to Yeovil Pen Mill

YT   Yeovil Town
YPM   Yeovil Pen Mill
YJ   Yeovil Junction

© Foxline

Lyng Halt, 16th May 1965. Lyng Halt, between the villages of East and West Lyng, was a halt opened on the section of the original Taunton-Yeovil line which had been bypassed by the cut-off from Athelney to Cogload Junction (which runs across the distant background of this view). 4575 Class 2-6-2T No. **4593** is arriving with the 12.37pm Yeovil Pen Mill-Taunton train.

M.J.Fox

Athelney, 30th May 1964. 4575 Class 2-6-2T No. **4591** arriving on the 2.10pm SO Taunton-Yeovil Pen Mill train. The single line to Durston diverges to the right behind the train. As this train travelled via Durston the signalman is waiting to collect the token.   ***R.A.Lumber***

Athelney, 14th August 1963. 57XX Class 0-6-0PT No. **9635** arriving on the 12.58pm Taunton-Yeovil Pen Mill.   ***M.J.Fox***

Curry Rivel Junction, 13th June 1964. Standard 3MT 2-6-2T No. **82040** takes the 12.58pm Taunton-Yeovil train off the main line on the final day on which a passenger service operated.

R.A.Lumber

Langport West, 11th April 1962. Langport West, on the Taunton-Yeovil line, was the earlier of Langport's two stations to be opened. 57XX Class 0-6-0PT No. **3669** stands with the 4.15pm Taunton-Yeovil Pen Mill train.

R.A.Lumber

Thorney and Kingsbury Halt, 15th June 1959. 4575 Class "Small Prairie" 2-6-2T No. **5571** rolls into the halt with a Taunton-Yeovil train.

R.J.Sellick

Martock, 23rd July 1958. Martock station had staggered Up and Down platforms, as shown by these two views taken from the footbridge. Here 4575 *R.C.Riley*
Class 2-6-2T No. **5563** runs in with a train from Yeovil.

Martock, 16th May 1965. Standard Class 3MT 2-6-2T No. **82044** arriving with the 4.25pm Taunton-Yeovil Pen Mill. Notice the platform shelter of characteristic Bristol & Exeter style.   *M.J.Fox*

Montacute, 13th June 1964. 4575 Class 2-6-2T No. **4593** calling with the 4.10pm Yeovil Pen Mill-Taunton.   *Hugh Ballantyne*

Montacute, c.1962. Looking along the platform past the signal box towards Yeovil. At this date the goods loop and cattle pens siding was still in use. The signal box was the second box at this station being opened on the 6th March 1908. The old box was situated half way along the loop on the main line side.   *R.T.H.Platt*

(Centre) Montacute, c.1962. A general view of the main station buildings and signal box. Due to staff shortages in the late fifties-early sixties the station was used as a halt. This caused the block section to be from Hendford to Martock with Montacute signal box being cut out. Within the frame in the signal box was a white paint lever which, when moved, dis-connected the interlocking mechanism within the frame enabling all Montacute signals for both directions to be released to the 'off' position. When goods trains had to call at the station to perform shunting the block section was restored. The yard was then worked by means of a ground frame at the east end. This was unlocked and locked by means of the key end of the single-line token which the driver had obtained from either the Hendford or Martock signalman before enterting the section.   *R.T.H.Platt*

(Below) Montacute, 18th May 1964. Standard Class 3MT 2-6-2T No. **82042** is waiting with the 9.45am Taunton-Yeovil Pen Mill train. The siding had been lifted and the signal box closed. Now the trackbed is utilised for a link road from Yeovil to the A303.   *R.A.Lumber*

Hendford Halt, 12th April 1962. This halt, opened during the 1930s, was on the outskirts of Yeovil near the Westland aircraft works. Ironically, Hendford had been the original Yeovil terminus of the line from Durston, before it was extended to Pen Mill. 45XX Class 2-6-2T No. **4507** halts with the 4.00pm Yeovil Pen Mill-Taunton.
R.A.Lumber

(Below) Yeovil Town, 6th September 1964. In this panoramic view the station platforms appear empty but the yard of the SR loco depot, code 72C, is quite crowded with a variety of locos of SR and BR standard types.
M.J.Fox

Yeovil Town, 19th April 1963. After the withdrawal of push-pull fitted M7 0-4-4Ts, and the transfer of Yeovil GW shed to the Southern Region, WR auto-trains took over the Yeovil Town-Yeovil Junction service. 54XX Class 0-6-0PT No. **5416** is standing at Yeovil Town with such a train.

M.J.Fox

G.W.R.

YEOVIL TOWN

Yeovil Pen Mill, 23rd June 1962. 54XX Class 0-6-0PT No. **5416** with two push-pull trailers leaving Pen Mill and passing the Up Branch inner home, with the Sunday 5.52pm auto-train to Yeovil Town. On the right are the main lines to Yeovil South Junction and Weymouth.   *G.D.King*

Yeovil Pen Mill, 14th March 1964. SR Class U 2-6-0 No. **31792** after arrival with the 9.45am train from Taunton. It is not, as might appear, standing in a bay platform but in the Main Up platform which provides access to both sides of the train.

P.W.Gray

Yeovil Pen Mill, 6th September 1964. A view of the station from the A30 road bridge. Whilst a DMU is leaving with the 2.00pm Bristol Temple Meads-Weymouth service, 64XX Class 0-6-0PT No. **6430** waits with a connecting auto-train to Yeovil Town, the date being subsequent to cessation of the Yeovil Pen Mill-Taunton service. From that time these services operated from Yeovil Town to both Junction and Pen Mill.

M.J.Fox

(Above) Yeovil Pen Mill, c.1960. A view of the junction at the south end of the station. To the right was the branch to Yeovil Town and that on the left was the Weymouth line. In the fork of the lines lies the shed, while the cattle pens are to the left. Class 57XX No. 4624 is seen on the Down Main.   *R.T.H.Platt*

(Centre) Yeovil Pen Mill, c.1960. At the south end of the station a view looking north along the Up platform towards the main station buildings. The interior of the station was a rather gloomy place on the best of days.   *R.T.H.Platt*

(Below) Yeovil Pen Mill, c.1960. A view at the north end of the station showing the signal box and the goods shed. The signal box shown was the replacement box built in 1937 to replace the original north and south boxes. This new box had a 65 lever frame and its construction required alterations to the track layout at the north end of the station.   *R.T.H.Platt*

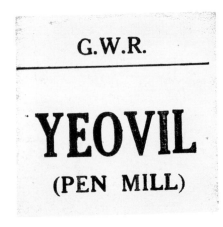

G.W.R.

YEOVIL

(PEN MILL)

Castle Cary Junction-Cogload Junction.

The origins of the line were explained earlier, namely that it was part of a new direct route to the West of England completed in 1906. The line passed through low rolling hills from Castle Cary and through Somerton tunnel to Langport where it descended into the Levels.

There were in fact two new sections, Castle Cary to Curry Rivell Junction, and from Athelney to Cogload Junction linked by an existing section of the Durston-Yeovil line which was upgraded. The latter mentioned new section was very short and involved no new stations or goods facilities.

Several stations were opened on the Castle Cary-Curry Rivell Junction stretch, and these were of the standard GWR designs of the period. Thus buildings at the larger stations were of GWR red and blue brick with flat roof on which rested a large canopy which gave protection to building as well as platform.

There were also more modest stations such as the simple halt later opened at Alford, and Long Sutton & Pitney station which had one of the "pagoda" waiting shelters on each platform.

The Taunton-Castle Cary local service was withdrawn in 1962, resulting in the closure of intermediate stations between Curry Rivell Junction and Castle Cary.

Castle Cary, c.1962. A view from a train looking along the tracks towards the junction, the left lines going to Yeovil Pen Mill and the right lines to Curry Rivel Junction and Taunton. At this date the loop behind the Down platform was still in use being taken out of use in 1963 leaving only a siding. Note the sign "Castle Carry Junction for Somerton Langport & Taunton". The original signal box, which was opened on 11 April 1905, was damaged during the last war and the new replacement box, which can just be seen in the distance, was built on the Up side of the line and opened on 27th October 1942. By the end of June 1969 the goods road together with the adjacent back siding had been taken out of use. In May 1968 the Weymouth branch was singled.

R.T.H.Platt

Castle Cary, 2nd July 1955. Looking west, with standard Class 7MT (Britannia) 4-6-2 No. **70017** *Arrow* passing with an express from the West Country to Paddington.

R.C.Riley

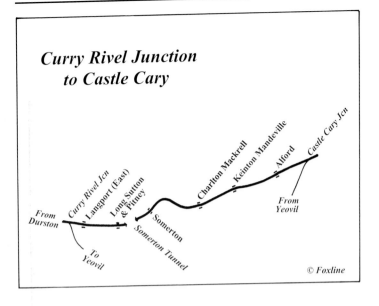

Curry Rivel Junction to Castle Cary

© *Foxline*

(Above Right) Alford Halt, c.1950's. A view looking east towards Castle Cary. The halt was devoid of any form of shelter and only had one ramp on each platform at the over bridge end. Further up the line was Alford signal box, opened 15th September 1940, to serve the War Department sidings on the Down side of the line. The connection was taken out of use and lifted on 8th April 1962. *Lens of Sutton*

Keinton Mandeville, c.1950's. A view looking east towards Castle Cary. The station was in an attractive area of the flat Somerset countryside surrounded by a copse of trees.
Lens of Sutton

Keinton Mandeville, c.1950's. Another view looking in the same direction, but from the opposite platform. *Lens of Sutton*

(Above) Charlton Mackrell, 10th April 1962. Standard 3MT 2-6-2T No. **82030** on the 8.55am Taunton-Castle Cary. The station was located in an attractive location and had on its platforms well attended flower beds and gardens. When open the station layout was nearly identical to that of Kinton Mandeville. In 1960 the main lines crossover together with the main line connections at the east end of the station platforms were removed The Sectional Appendix contained a reference to the station. With the station having no loops or refuge sidings there was a instruction that stated "*trains conveying passengers were permitted to be shunted from one running line to another for more important trains to be allowed to pass, when necessary, to avoid serious delay.*" By the time of closure on 10th September 1962 the summer timetable was showing 3 Down trains (SX) , 2 (SO) and 4 Up trains (SX), 3(SO) that stopped at the station. The signal box closed in December 1963. *R.A.Lumber*

Charlton Mackrell, c.1910. An early undated view, looking west and showing the well kept gardens on the station platforms which it was noted for. *Lens of Sutton*

Somerton, undated. Looking east. The nameboard is lettered SOMERTON som, presumably to distinguish it from Somertons in Norfolk or Oxfordshire, though neither of those had railway stations. The station layout as originally built was again similar to those at Charlton Mackrell and Keinton Mandeville, but in 1929 with the opening of a new milk factory close by, a loading ramp was constructed along side the goods shed siding to handle this additional traffic from the factory. In June/July 1943 wartime loops were constructed to the west of the station to handle the increase in traffic. Each loop was capable of holding 86 wagons plus engine and brake. Both loops were taken out of use in March/April 1951.

Lens of Sutton

(Below) Long Sutton and Pitney, 8th October 1952. 90XX Class (Dukedog) 4-4-0 struggles past on a long Up freight train. *R.A. Lumber*

Long Sutton and Pitney, 14th April 1962. Warship Diesel-Hydraulic No. **D803** *Albion* on the 2.30pm Paddington-Plymouth passing Long Sutton goods yard.

M.J.Fox

Langport East, 11th April 1962. With the opening of the Castle Cary-Curry Rivell cut-off, Langport gained a second station. 51XX Class 2-6-2T No. **5180** on the 3.45pm Taunton-Castle Cary.

R.A.Lumber

Creech Junction- Chard Junction

The first railway to reach Chard was opened in 1863, a branch from Chard Junction on the LSWR Waterloo-Exeter line (at that time named Chard Road) to a station named Chard Town. The Bristol & Exeter had not initially shown much interest in Chard, but this changed with the appearance in the town of the standard gauge rival and, after purchase by the B&E of the Chard Canal, a broad-gauge branch was opened in 1866, quickly followed by closure of the canal. The branch ran through undulating country with moderate gradients, and one tunnel near Hatch.

The broad-gauge branch was from Creech Junction ,about 2 miles east of Taunton, to a station ultimately known as Chard Central, though on the north-east edge of the town. The LSWR also built a spur from its own branch from Chard Junction, to a bay platform at the GWR station to provide through connections. After the GWR branch was regauged in 1891 through running between Taunton and Chard Junction became possible, and in 1896 the GWR took over responsibility for maintenance of the line to Chard Town, which was placed under the GWR stationmaster. It was some time before complete rationalisation took place, but during the First World War Chard Town was closed to passenger traffic and the GWR took over the workings between Chard Joint (as its station had been renamed) and Chard Junction. After a time the timetable was recast to allow through working between Taunton and Chard Junction, and in 1928 the track to the bay platform at Chard station was lifted. Even in BR days many trains had a lengthy wait at Chard Central before proceeding to Junction as a nominally separate train.

The original buildings on the Chard branch are worthy of note. Hatch, Ilminster and Chard Central retained classic Brunel-period chalet-style buildings to the end, Chard being complete with an overall roof. Ilminster's features included a commodious goods shed and a loading gauge with wrought iron embellishments, and Hatch's broad-gauge origins were evident in the clearances of the bridge which crossed the yard.

In contrast Thornfalcon, which was not opened until 1871, had a tiny wooden station whereas, of the two halts opened in 1928 to counter bus competition, Donyatt Halt had just a waiting

hut, and Ilton Halt no shelter at all.

The branch was rather unusual in that none of the stations were able to cross two passenger trains. There were loops at Creech Junction and immediately north of Chard Central, but the loops at Hatch and Ilminster had platform on one side only and were solely used to cross goods and passenger trains.

Apart from the long waits at Chard Central resulting from the need to afford mainline connections at both ends of the journey there appears little to say about the services. "Metro" 2-4-0Ts were a favourite motive power in earlier days, but later the normal motive power was class 45XX, or else 57XX after the latter had been reclassified from "blue" to "yellow" route restriction in 1950. Taunton's solitary 74XX pannier, initially No. 7421, later replaced by 7436, also seemed to be favoured for Chard trains.

The line was the first of Taunton's branches to close, officially from Monday 10th September 1962. There being no Sunday service, the last train ran on the evening of Saturday 8th, the author being one of the passengers.

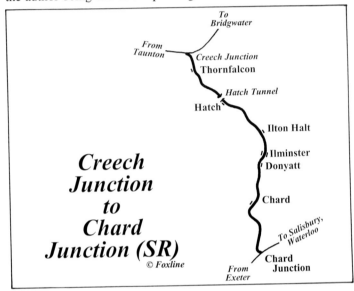

Thornfalcon, 16th June 1962. Sometimes referred to as Thorne, the location of this station was at the southern end of the village of Henlade, outside Taunton. Its wooden buildings bore no similarity to the other stations on the line. The lorry and the warehouse behind it bear the name G. Small and Sons, a firm of coal, corn and lime merchants who, at that date, had operated from the site for well over 60 years. The train is the 8.00am Taunton-Chard, headed by 57XX Class 0-6-0PT No. **3787.**   *M.J.Fox*

Hatch, 9th June 1961. The clearance under the arches of the bridge demonstrates that the line was originally laid to broad gauge. 74XX Class 0-6-0PT No. **7436** continues towards its destination of Chard Junction with the 4.07pm train from Taunton. Through the arch of the road bridge can be seen the goods shed in front of which was the cattle dock which, by this date, had been converted into a loading ramp. On the 23rd September 1956 the goods loop was taken out of use and the signal box closed. At the same date a ground frame, just off the picture to the left, was brought into use to control entrance to the goods yard. As a result of the removal of the goods loop, the loading gauge was removed and resited on the siding to the left of the goods shed road.

M.J.Fox

Hatch, undated. A view looking towards Chard, showing the Brunel-chalet station buildings of a mellow brickwork and arched windows with a low pitched roof, a style repeated at Ilminster and Chard Central. Here the village's full name is Hatch Beauchamp. The cast iron letters on the name board dated from Bristol & Exeter days and lasted until the closure of the line. The signal box was located on the side of the goods loop opposite the goods shed. If one looked in the other direction down the platform the mouth of the 152 yard long Hatch tunnel would be seen. This tunnel was originally built to accommodate a double track but the branch traffic never warranted the doubling of the line. *Lens of Sutton*

Ilton Halt, c.1950's. An undated photograph which shows the very basic halt and the lack of any shelter or waiting facilities although a seat has been provided. A notice board presumably gives train information at this halt. The access to the halt was via a narrow path, which in winter was more often than not rather muddy.
Lens of Sutton

(Centre) Ilminster, c.1962. A view looking towards Chard, showing the station buildings which were of the same design as those at Hatch. The area that the station served was agricultural being reflected in the goods traffic that was received, mainly that of cattle feed for distribution in the local area and coal. There was little goods traffic out but even so it had a staff of seven.
G.H.Platt

(Below) Ilminster, 24th March 1962. A view of the station and goods yard, with 57XX Class 0-6-0PT No. **3787** leaving with the 3.20pm train from Taunton to Chard. Notice the range of vintage buildings, including a large goods shed and loading gauge of standard GW pattern but with exceptionally elaborate embellishments.
M.J.Fox

Donyatt Halt, 1st September 1961. 4575 Class 2-6-2T No. **5571** coasts in with the 2.50pm train from Taunton to Chard Central. *M.J.Fox*

Chard Central, 2nd July 1956. Beneath the overall roof looking towards Taunton. The train is the 1.35pm to Taunton, comprising "B set" coaches W6999/7000W and 8750 Class 0-6-0PT No. **4604.**
Hugh Ballantyne

Chard Central, 6th July 1961. 74XX Class 0-6-0PT No. **7436** waits for departure time with train for Chard Junction   *R.C.Riley*

Chard Central, 9th June 1961. After arrival at Chard Central, the 2.50pm from Taunton faced a long pause before continuing as the 4.07pm Chard Central-Chard Junction. 57XX Class 0-6-0PT No. **9718** departs on this train. In earlier times trains between the two Chard stations would only have used the bay platform which can be seen, overgrown, in this picture.   *M.J.Fox*

Chard Town, 6th July 1961. This, the original terminus of the LSWR line from Chard Junction, was closed to passengers from 1st January 1917, and thereafter used only as a goods depot.

R.C.Riley

Chard Junction, 10th February 1962. As shown here, the branch platform was quite separate from the main line station on the right. 4575 Class 2-6-2T No. **5554** stands with the 12.45pm departure to Chard Central.

P.W.Gray

Taunton-Tiverton Junction

Above a retaining wall on the west side of Station Road, and on the west side of the road between its crossing by the goods loop and the passenger station, stood the new loco depot constructed at the same time as the goods loop, in 1896. It occupied a roughly triangular site, tapering towards Taunton West Junction, which incorporated carriage sidings as well as tracks where engines could be stored.

Beyond Taunton West Junction, on the Down side of the line was Fairwater Yard, put in during the Second World War, and stretching as far as Silk Mill level crossing. On the Down side between Silk Mill and Norton Fitzwarren was Blinkhorn Yard, serving a large War Department (later Ministry of Defence) depot.

At Norton Fitzwarren, which had started life as Watchet Junction when the West Somerset line was built, the Minehead and Barnstaple branches left the main line. The latter then began its climb out of the Vale of Taunton Deane up Wellington bank, down which "City of Truro" achieved its legendary speed of 102 mph, or was it really only 99? - in 1904. Above Wellington, where banking engines were stationed, the gradient steepens to 1 in 90, and at Beam Bridge, temporary terminus of the B&E whilst Whiteball Tunnel was being bored, 1 in 81. At the summit of the bank the line passes under a shoulder of the Blackdown Hills by means of the tunnel, crossing into Devon in the process. Beyond the tunnel at Whiteball siding were a loop and refuges, and a crossover to allow banking engines to cross to the Up line before returning to their base at Wellington.

Once out of Whiteball tunnel the gradients are downhill all the way to Exeter, as the line follows the Sampford stream, then the Culm and finally the Exe. For up trains the climb to Whiteball Tunnel is longer, but less severe than for down trains.

Before reaching Tiverton Junction there were small stations at Burlescombe, Sampford Peverell Halt. The former used to have a GWR-owned 3ft gauge feeder line to Westleigh Quarries, where railway ballast was quarried. This was opened in 1875 and converted to standard gauge in 1898. Sampford Peverell Halt was opened in 1928; like

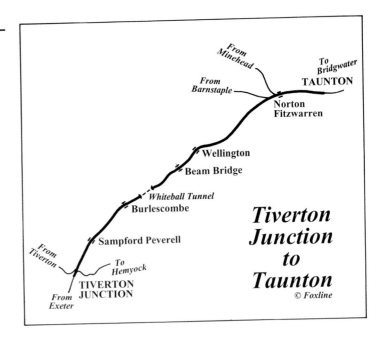

Wellington after its rebuilding, it had through roads between the platform roads for non-stop traffic. After Tiverton Junction was extended there were two island platforms as well as two central through roads for non-stop trains. The outer faces of the two island platforms served the two branches, to Hemyock and to Tiverton; and there was an engine shed (subshed to Exeter, EXE, 83C), which accommodated two 14XX Class 0-4-2T locomotives, one for each branch. After Exeter's steam shed closed, the Tiverton Junction subshed was transferred to Taunton for the brief remainder of its life.

The Tiverton-Tiverton Junction service ceased in October 1964, and the intermediate stations on the Norton Fitzwarren-Tiverton Junction section of the main line were closed from the same date. In May 1986 Tiverton Junction station was replaced by the new "Tiverton Parkway" built on the site of Sampford Peverell Halt. The former Tiverton Junction station itself still stands derelict in 1991.

Taunton, 5th July 1946. 54XX auto-fitted 0-6-0PT No. **5406** takes water at the incoming end of platform 7 during a break in carriage shunting. The water column would have been more commonly used from the other side, by an engine which had arrived with a branch train to No. 8 bay. *J.Alves*

Taunton, c.1955. The Down departure bays and Taunton loco shed in the background with: In platform 3, 4575 Class 2-6-2T No. **5558** on a train for Barnstaple; in platform 4 sister No. **5503** on a train for Minehead; in the coach siding behind, 57XX Class 0-6-0PT No. **9647**. Note the "B" and "M" destination targets on the two branch trains.

Lens of Sutton

Taunton, July 1947. 2251 Class No. **2214** (Taunton Shed) is seen waiting to depart with a Barnstable branch train from the No. 3 bay platform (west end of station). Also in the bay platform No. 4 is a Minehead branch train behind 5100 Class No. **4113**. The bay platforms were mainly used by these branch trains, but both were also used by Taunton to Exeter stopping trains.

R.A. Venning

(Below) Taunton West Junction, September 1946. Ex. Burry Port & Gwendraeth Valley Railway 0-6-0ST No. **2194** *Kidwelly* seen shunting under the Fairwater bridge just west of Taunton West Junction.

R.A. Venning

Norton Fitzwarren, c.1910. An old view looking towards Exeter before quadrupling. The view shows a fine collection of enamel signs there being
two of them advertising Pears Soap.   *Lens of Sutton*

Norton Fitzwarren, 29th September 1962. 43XX Class 2-6-0 No. **7325** passing through the station with an Up Class H main line freight. *M.J.Fox*

Norton Fitzwarren, 19th August 1961. On this summer Saturday,the services were disrupted by the derailment of a banking engine at Whiteball, causing trains to be blocked back at least as far as Norton Fitzwarren. Four Down main line trains were visible from the station footbridge, including one headed by Warship No. **D800** *Sir Brian Robertson*. The Minehead branch can be seen diverging to the right, also the Barnstaple branch (right background).

M.J.Fox

Norton Fitzwarren, 19th August 1961. Obviously the hasty substitute from another failure the same day, Swindon's 49XX Class 4-6-0 No. **5978** *Bodinnick Hall* waits in the queue on the Down Torbay Express.

M.J.Fox

Victory Siding, 22nd December 1962. 43XX Class 2-6-0 No. **7337** approaches the foot of Wellington bank on a Down freight. The little siding here *M.J.Fox*
was adjacent to the Grand Western Canal by the Victory Inn at Allerford.

Wellington (Somerset), 6th July 1957. 4073 Class (Castle) 4-6-0
No. **5074** *Hampden* rushes through on the fast line with the Up Torbay
Express.   *R.C.Riley*

Wellington (Somerset), 26th September 1958. An unidentified 60XX King Class 4-6-0 passes through the station on the Down main with the 9.30am Paddington-Plymouth train. Meanwhile banking engine 51XX Class 2-6-2T No. **4128** stands in the bay; it is possibly coupled to the passenger brake van, and waiting for departure to Tiverton Junction to collect milk tankers in transit from Hemyock Dairy.

R.J.Sellick

Wellington (Somerset), 4th August 1955. Expresses cross at Wellington; 4073 Class (Castle) 4-6-0 No. **7000** *Viscount Portal* on the Down Devonian and two 4-6-0s double heading the 12 noon Penzance - Crewe; Modified Hall No. **6996** *Blackwell Hall* and No. **5038** *Morlais Castle.*

P.W.Gray

(Above) Wellington Bank, 26th Jan 1963. Standard 3MT 2-6-2T No. **82008** drifts down the bank at Beam Bridge on a Tiverton Junction -Taunton goods train   *M.J.Fox*

Wellington Bank, 10th August 1962. 28XX Class 2-8-0 No. **3848**, banked by 49XX Class 4-6-0 No. **4922** *Envill Hall*, on a down freight.   *M.J.Fox*

(Below) Whiteball, 18th August 1962. 49XX Class 4-6-0 No. **5945** *Leckhampton Hall* leaving the Devon portal of the tunnel on a SO Manchester -Penzance train.

M.J.Fox

(Above) Whiteball Siding, 4th August 1962. 4073 Class (Castle) 4-6-0 No. **5076** *Gladiator* passes the signal box with a 9.30am Paddington-Newquay relief. Behind the engine is a refuge siding added in 1904 for banking engines waiting to return to Wellington. In October 1972 this was taken out of use. The signal box was damaged by fire on the 28th November 1958 and a temporary box was erected on the Up line side until the original was brought back into use. *M.J.Fox*

Whiteball Siding, 11th August 1961. 4073 Class 4-6-0 No. **4075** *Cardiff Castle* on a Friday down empty stock train comprising dining cars for the Saturday up services. The train is passing over the point work of the Down Relief line which was installed in July 1927. In July 1966 this was reduced to a Down loop before being taken out of use in 1985. *M.J.Fox*

Burlescombe, 2nd July 1955. 49XX Class 4-6-0 No. **6946** *Heatherden Hall* passing through the station on the 9.15am Liverpool - Plymouth.   *R.C.Riley*

Burlescombe, 4th August 1962. Three 3-car Swindon DMUs with Bristol TM destination blind, but probably the 7.45am Newton Abbot - Cardiff, passing
Burlescombe goods yard. This was earlier the interchange point from the narrow gauge Westleigh Quarry tramway.   *M.J.Fox*

Burlescombe, 10th June 1957. A characteristic sight of that period, Taunton 68XX Class 4-6-0 No. **6874** *Haughton Grange* on its way to Tiverton Junction to pick up a milk train for London. ***M.J.Fox***

(Centre) Sampford Peverell Halt, 31st July 1954. On this date 49XX Class No. **4914** *Cranmore Hall* on the 10.55am Paignton-Nottingham failed at Burlescombe with a collapsed brick arch. The 7.30am Penzance-Wolverhampton headed by 4073 Class No. **5077** *Fairey Battle* waits on the Up through road as 60XX Class 4-6-0 No. **6001** *King Edward VII* creeps into the Up platform road with the 8.15am Perranporth-Paddington. ***P.W.Gray***

(Below) Sampford Peverell Halt, 26th September 1958. An unidentified King Class 4-6-0 passing through on the Up main with the Penzance-Paddington "Cornish Riviera Express". ***R.J.Sellick***

Tiverton Junction, 21st December 1963. With a light covering of snow on the ground 49XX Class 4-6-0 No. **5992** *Horton Hall* is entering the station with an oil train for the oil storage depot visible behind the train. The line diverging out of the picture from the right hand platform is the Culm Valley branch. *M.J.Fox*

(Below) **Tiverton Junction, 11th May 1957.** This view of the Down side platforms shows two 14XX Class 0-4-2T locos drawn up side by side. At the rear is No. **1429** waiting departure with a Hemyock train, but more puzzling is the train standing in the main-line platform behind No. **1440**. It does not appear to be the Tiverton train, as there is no access to the branch from this platform. Moreover the train comprises two trailers not one, and they are of the end-entrance "suburban" type used in the then Plymouth district, not the "branch" type with central door and collapsable steps. *M.J.Fox*

Tiverton Junction, 15th June 1962. A view looking down towards Exeter, with 43XX Class 2-6-0 No. **7311** arriving on an Exeter-Taunton stopping train. The small Tiverton Junction loco shed (for Culm Valley and 'Tivvy Bumper" locos) is behind the eaves of the platform building, to the right of the signal box.

R.C.Riley

Tiverton Junction, 8th August 1962. 4073 Class (Castle) 4-6-0 No. **5075** *Wellington* passes through and, despite the reporting number, the train has been identified as being an empty stock working whilst a goods train headed by a 28XX Class is held in the platform road.

M.J.Fox

Norton Fitzwarren Junction – Minehead

The Minehead branch was built in two stages several years apart. The first objective, reached in 1862, had simply been the port of Watchet, the extension to Minehead being opened in 1874 as the Minehead Railway. These two phases are clearly reflected in the architecture of the line. Between Bishops Lydeard and Watchet all the stations are neat and plain chalets of ashlar sandstone blocks. Beyond Watchet the stations at Washford, Dunster and Minehead are of a more ornate Victorian gothic cottage style built of coursed sandstone rubble with limestone facings. The varied group of buildings at Blue Anchor have no equivalent elsewhere on the line. They may date from 1904 when the loop was put in.

The Minehead branch benefited from the government-subsidised programme of works put through during the 1930s, in order to combat the depression. The capacity of the branch to deal with holiday traffic had been hampered by the fact that only Bishops Lydeard, Crowcombe, Williton and Blue Anchor could cross passenger trains. The branch was therefore doubled from Minehead to Dunster in 1934, and from the junction to Bishops Lydeard in 1936. Two new loops were created in open country during 1933; Leigh Bridge near Stogumber and Kentsford near Watchet. Platforms at several stations were also lengthened during the same decade.

The line was closed to goods traffic in 1964 but passenger services survived until 1971. Butlin's camp at Minehead maintained the holiday traffic beyond the end of steam, when the branch saw North British type 2 and Hymek diesel-hydraulics as well as DMU's.

The Minehead line is more severely graded than the branches we have depicted so far. There are climbs as steep as 1 in 65 to Washford, where the line has to run behind the cliffs between Blue Anchor and Watchet, another climb where the line leaves the sea between Watchet and Williton, and a long climb at around 1 in 100 in both directions to Crowcombe at the foot of the Quantock Hills. However, the work done during the 1930s enabled Minehead to accept "Blue" restriction engines as well as a more intensive service at holiday weekends. The consequence is that Minehead saw a greater variety of power than did other branches:- 43XX 2-6-0, 51XX/61XX 2-6-2T, 2251 0-6-0, 45XX 2-6-2T, 57XX 0-6-0PT. Some of the 45XX workings were of Yeovil engines, diagrams requiring them to work from Taunton to Minehead and back before returning to Yeovil.

Happily, the branch now operates as the West Somerset Railway Ltd between Minehead and Bishops Lydeard, the company having being incorporated within a few months of closure by BR. The line was reopened from Minehead to Williton in 1976, and to Bishops Lydeard in 1979. A through service to Taunton remains a possibilty, although initial objections of NUR bus crews remained a problem for some time; their union affiliation itself being a historical relic of the divesting from the GWR of its bus services to form the Western National bus group.

Loss of the loops at Crowcombe, Leigh Bridge and Kentsford was keenly missed, and access to the main line, was only be made via the Taunton Cider Company's siding into which the WSR has been diverted at Norton. However, the loop at

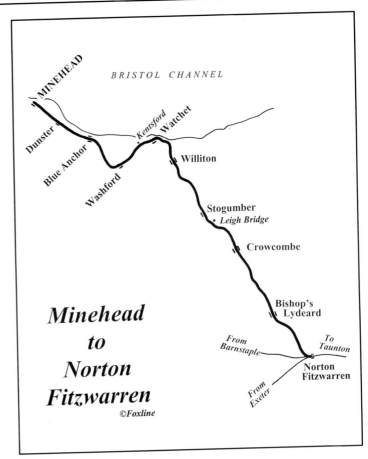

Minehead to Norton Fitzwarren

©Foxline

Crowcombe station has subsequently been re-laid and resignalled, and negotiations have continued over the intervening years to regain access to Taunton. A new halt was opened at Doniford Beach between Williton and Watchet in 1988 for seasonal use.

Apart from Minehead itself several of the intermediate stations have developed their own interest for visitors; the Diesel and Electric group at Williton, the Somerset and Dorset Trust at Washford, a small GWR museum at Blue Anchor, a display of broad-gauge trackwork at Crowcombe and a model railway club at Bishop's Lydeard The West Somerset Railway Association headquarters is to be found at Bishop's Lydeard. My personal opinion is that Williton station remains the most fascinating relic. Being more extensive, as befitted one of the largest villages en route, it has retained all its old structures except the footbridge and water tower; the Bristol & Exeter signal box is of particular interest.

Bishops Lydeard, 22nd August 1964. The 8.10am SO Taunton-Minehead train arriving at the station, up to which point the branch was doubled during the 1930s. The exceptional length of the train is due to its forming two return workings from Minehead; the 9.25am to Manchester and the 9.45am to Taunton. The locos are North British Locomotive Co. type 2 Diesel-Hydraulic No. **D6336** and 61XX Class 2-6-2T No. **6148.** *M.J.Fox*

7 DAYS' UNLIMITED TRAVEL
THE WEST COUNTRY

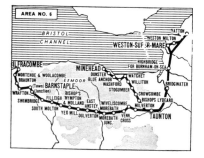

Crowcombe, c.1910. This early view is looking towards Taunton. The station is located at Crowcombe Heathfield, almost two miles from the village. Note the use of track materials which comprise former broad gauge components of bridge rail on longitudinal baulks of timber, dating from the conversion of the branch in 1882. *Lens of Sutton*

Crowcombe, 29th August 1961. 4575 Class 2-6-2T No. **4593** leaving with the 9.03am Minehead-Taunton train. The cutting at Crowcombe marks the highest point of the Minehead Branch.
M.J.Fox

Leigh Bridge Loop, 3rd June 1962. One of the two loops built during the 1930s to increase line capacity, Leigh Bridge was between Crowcombe and Stogumber. 51XX Class 2-6-2T No. **4110** is hauling the 4.45pm Taunton-Minehead.
M.J.Fox

Stogumber, c.1950's. Visible in this photograph is a milk tanker, converted to supply drinking water, which arrived on site every spring to provide Stogumber water supply for the station and the camping coach. The camping coach can be seen in the siding, together with the tanker, at the far end of the station. In the early 1950's the camping coach was a 55ft. clerestory composite. Due to the lack of station buildings there was a stores van provided for the storage of fresh linen and other requisites. Also in the view is the wooden platform which overhung the embankment. Present day travellers on the West Somerset Railway will notice a similarity with this scene having witnessed a progressive resurrection from the abandonment and dereliction of the 1970's to a well restored and used railway. *Lens of Sutton*

Stogumber, 24th August 1963. Standard 3MT 2-6-2T No. **82042** passing with the 12.07pm SO Minehead-Cardiff. The picture shows the lack of space on the west side of the track which required the station building to be sited on the opposite side of the line to the platform. By this date the camping coach had been changed to a 57ft TK . The water tanker and stores van can also be seen to the far end of the siding. *P.W.Gray*

Williton, 24th August 1963. Castle Hill, where the line crosses the A358 road, has become a favourite spot for photographers on the West Somerset Railway. In earlier times 51XX Class 2-6-2T No. **4143** is heading the 2.20pm Minehead-Paddington on a climb which will not end until Crowcombe.   *P.W.Gray*

Williton, 22nd August 1964. The DMU forming the 8.17am Minehead-Taunton is crossing the 8.10am Taunton-Minehead train also depicted in this book at Bishops Lydeard. The attractive collection of buildings at Williton includes a B&E signal box which still operates on the preserved line.   *M.J.Fox*

Watchet, 22nd August 1964. Hymek type 3 Diesel-Hydraulic No. **D7094** leaving Watchet on the 9.43am Taunton-Minehead. The station building is aligned at right angles to the track, Watchet being the original terminus of the branch.

M.J.Fox

G. W. R.

WATCHET

(Below) **Watchet, 12th September 1951.** 57XX Class 0-6-0PT No. **5798** shunts the harbour sidings. It is low tide and the harbour has dried out, temporarily stranding the *SS Margol*.

R.J.Sellick

Watchet, 24th August 1963. Hymek type 3 Diesel-Hydraulic No. **D7007** passing through Watchet with the 10.15am SO Paddington-Minehead. Behind the train are the sidings of the Wansbrough Paper Company. The bridge that the train is passing over carried the line over the old track bed of the West Somerset Mineral Railway to Watchet harbour. This was finally closed in March 1910. *P.W.Gray*

(Below) Kentsford Loop, 23rd December 1949. A view of the signal box looking up towards Watchet. Note the automatic token exchanging apparatus. This is the other loop, in addition to Leigh Bridge, which was put in during the 1930's to improve the traffic handling capacity of the line. Previously there was no provision for crossing passenger trains between Williton and Blue Anchor. *R.J.Sellick*

(Above) Washford, 9th June 1962. 51XX Class 2-6-2T No. **4103** restarts the 2.40pm Taunton-Minehead train from the station which is now, on the West Somerset Railway, the headquarters of the Somerset & Dorset Railway Trust, and the home of their collection of rolling stock and S&DJR artefacts. *M.J.Fox*

Washford, 2nd September 1961. 43XX Class 2-6-0 No. **6378** rolls over the summit into the station, on the 12.20pm SO Minehead-Wolverhampton train, composed on this occasion of LNER stock. *M.J.Fox*

Both **Washford** and **Dunster** were scheduled stops on all local services. However, certain summer Saturday through workings in 1963 called at Dunster but missed out Washford. Nowadays it is perhaps worth reflecting that during the summer months there were through trains serving Minehead to and from Paddington (2), Manchester, Cardiff and Wolverhampton.

Dunster, c.1950's. A view looking towards Minehead. The double-track from Minehead, put in during the 1930s, finished just short of the station platform, since doubling the track through the station itself would have necessitated demolishing the goods shed. *Lens of Sutton*

(Above) Minehead, 29th August 1961. 57XX Class 0-6-0PT No. 5779 shunting the branch goods train. Notice that the GWR's signal box was on the opposite (seaward) side of the line to the replacement WSR signal box, which is now roughly where the photographer was standing.   *M.J.Fox*

Minehead, c.1950's. A view which illustrates the length of the platform in later years, after it had been extended to accommodate through holiday trains from Paddington and elsewhere.
                                                  Lens of Sutton

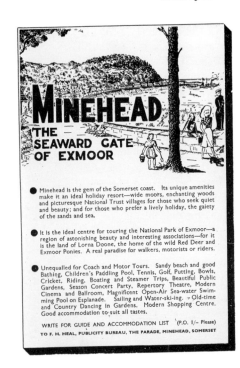

MINEHEAD
THE SEAWARD GATE OF EXMOOR

● Minehead is the gem of the Somerset coast. Its unique amenities make it an ideal holiday resort—wide moors, enchanting woods and picturesque National Trust villages for those who seek quiet and beauty; and for those who prefer a lively holiday, the gaiety of the sands and sea.

● It is the ideal centre for touring the National Park of Exmoor—a region of astonishing beauty and interesting associations—for it is the land of Lorna Doone, the home of the wild Red Deer and Exmoor Ponies. A real paradise for walkers, motorists or riders.

● Unequalled for Coach and Motor Tours. Sandy beach and good Bathing, Children's Paddling Pool, Tennis, Golf, Putting, Bowls, Cricket, Riding, Boating and Steamer Trips, Beautiful Public Gardens, Season Concert Party, Repertory Theatre, Modern Cinema and Ballroom, Magnificent Open-Air Sea-water Swimming Pool on Esplanade. Sailing and Water-ski-ing. Old-time and Country Dancing in Gardens. Modern Shopping Centre. Good accommodation to suit all tastes.

WRITE FOR GUIDE AND ACCOMMODATION LIST (P.O. 1/- Please)
TO F. H. HEAL, PUBLICITY BUREAU, THE PARADE, MINEHEAD, SOMERSET

Minehead, c.1950's. 2251 Class 0-6-0 No. 2213 standing with a train for Taunton.
                                                  Lens of Sutton

Norton Fitzwarren Junction-Barnstaple

This was the lengthiest of the Taunton branches (45 miles) and the most severe (ruling gradient 1 in 58). Skirting Exmoor it was also the most scenic, though the Minehead branch was a close rival. It started life as the Devon and Somerset Railway, being opened to a terminus at Barnstaple Victoria Road in 1873. In 1887 a connection was made to Barnstaple Junction, but only in BR days was Victoria Road abandoned, all trains then terminating at Barnstaple Junction, or else continuing to Ilfracombe or Torrington.

On the first section to be opened the two stations at Milverton and Wiveliscombe were of recognisable "H" plan style, similar to many B&E stations, but as building the line struggled on with another contractor this uniformity disappeared. Dulverton, (actually at Brushford, some couple of miles from Dulverton which was up a valley not leading towards Barnstaple), was the major intermediate centre and Exe Valley trains continued from Morebath Junction to terminate here. The Halt at Morebath Junction was opened in 1928. The line had a number of attractive viaducts and bridges of lattice deck girders with sandstone piers or approach arches. The largest of these were Tone (or Waterrow) and Castle Hill (or Filleigh) Viaducts.

Like the Minehead branch the services were seasonal because of the holiday traffic. In the summer the local trains would be strengthened by one or more extra coaches, often redundant slip coaches once the WR had abandoned slip services on mainline trains. Ilfracombe trains could be formed of SR corridor stock, and holiday trains of stock appropriate to their originating region. Apart from the pickup goods which ran from Taunton as far as South Molton, all services were handled by 43XX 2-6-0s, with the reluctant compliance of the Civil Engineer who restricted them to 15 mph over Tone and Castle Hill Viaducts. In earlier years Bulldog 4-4-0s handled much of the traffic, though these had left the district by 1950.

After closure of the Victoria Road sub-shed, Taunton engines spending the night at Barnstaple were serviced by Barnstaple Junction (72E). In the case of an engine failure, and at some periods on regular diagrams, SR engines worked to Taunton. These were normally examples of Class N 2-6-0, sometimes T9 4-4-0.

The line was doubled between Norton Fitzwarren and Milverton in 1937. Closure took place in 1966.

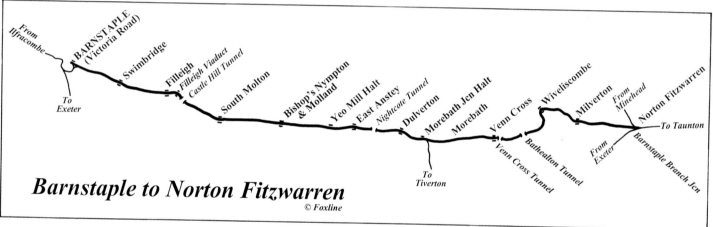

Barnstaple to Norton Fitzwarren

© Foxline

Milverton, 28th September 1963. 43XX Class 2-6-0 No. **7332** is working the 5.55pm Taunton - Barnstaple. When the loop was added in 1880 the Up platform was constructed longer than the orginal Down which was left as built. Further alterations to the track layout took place in 1925 and 1936. The goods yard was closed in May 1964 some two years before complete closure of the line.

Hugh Ballantyne

Milverton, 24th March 1962. 43XX Class 2-6-0 No. **6372** arriving with the 8.12am Barnstaple Junction-Taunton train. Notice, as in the case of Martock, the B&E shelter on the Up platform. The trackbed stretching away behind the train is now the route of the Milverton bypass and the A361 road.   *M.J.Fox*

EXPLORE SOMERSET . . .

WITH A

HOLIDAY RUNABOUT TICKET

★ THE CHEAPEST FORM OF HOLIDAY TRAVEL
★ UNLIMITED RAIL JOURNEYS IN CERTAIN AREAS
FOR **SEVEN DAYS**
★ ISSUED MAY TO OCTOBER

For further details see pages xxix to xxxi

Wiveliscombe, c.1950's. Many of the stations on the Devon and Somerset line were built on an "H" floorplan characteristic of the B&E. This view of the front of the station also shows two other modes of transport of the day, the bicycle and the moped. It should also be noted the flaking paintwork on the walls of the station together with the notice boards advertising cheap excursions.   *Lens of Sutton*

(Above) **Wiveliscombe, 28th August 1961.** 43XX Class 2-6-0 No. **7304** leaving on the 4.35pm Taunton-Bamstaple Junction. *M.J.Fox*

(Left) **Wiveliscombe, c.1965.** A view from the Down platform showing the station buildings and goods shed. In 1906 the platforms were lengthened and alterations to the layout of the goods yard also took place but leaving the goods shed in its original place. A new signal box was built in the position shown in the photograph whilst the original box, which was at the other end of the platform was demolished. *S.J.Dickson*

Wiveliscombe, c.1965. A further view from the Down platform showing the station buildings. These had changed little since they were built in 1871 with the exception of the addition of the wooden lean-to and the brick and stonework being painted white. From 1871 to 1873 Wiveliscombe was the terminus of the line. Interesting to note are the numerous fire buckets hanging on their stands. *S.J.Dickson*

Wiveliscombe, c.1965. A view of the signal box on the Up platform.   *S.J.Dickson*

Through the 1950's, the Western Region continued to embrace it's Taunton to Barnstaple service within a London (Paddington) to Ilfracombe umbrella, also including Dulverton because of the Exe Valley connection. During the summer of 1953, Wiveliscombe, like all the other stations on the line, had seven trains in each direction during the week. On Saturdays, there was an extra westbound train to Barnstaple Junction, which, for no apparent reason, took almost thirty minutes longer than the other services. Somewhat surprisingly, passengers alighting at Barnstaple Victoria Road station were still met by a Southern National Bus which provided connections with points on the erstwhile Lyton & Barnstaple line, closed almost two decades earlier. Wiveliscombe lost its passenger trains from the 3rd October 1966.

(Below) Wiveliscombe, 28th August 1961. 43XX Class 2-6-0 No. **6375** leaving on the 8.12am Barnstaple Junction-Taunton train. Beyond Wiveliscombe station down trains had to surmount the Brendon Hills, involving the climb to Bathealton Tunnel, descent to the Tone Viaduct at Waterrow, then another climb to Venn Cross Tunnel.
M.J.Fox

Tone Viaduct, Waterrow, 5th September 1964. Between the tunnels at Bathealton and Venn Cross, the line drops on gradients of 1 in 58 to bridge the River Tone. Trains were limited to 25mph over the viaduct, and for some time this was restricted to 15mph for the 43XX Class. Here No. **5336** of that Class crosses with train for Barnstaple.

M.J.Fox

(Left) Venn Cross, c.1965. By this date services were being operated by DMU's. However, seen here is a Pressed Steel Co. single unit railcar (Later Class 121) on the Taunton - Barnstaple service, in the process of exchanging token. By this date the connections into the goods yard had been lifted. **S.J.Dickson**

(Below) Venn Cross, 24th March 1962. 43XX Class 2-6-0 No. **6340** passing the simple goods yard as it runs to Venn Cross station, on the 10.02am Barnstaple Junction-Taunton train.

M.J.Fox

Venn Cross, 21st July 1961. 43XX Class 2-6-0 No. **7333** about to enter the tunnel at the head of an Up train composed of SR Bulleid stock. The unusual location and construction of the signal allows it to be sighted through the tunnel. The Devon & Somerset line actually crosses the county boundary at three points, one of which is Venn Cross station.

M.J.Fox

Morebath station, September 1962. This view of the station shows the loop still in situ six months before it was taken out of use and lifted. When the loop was taken out the signal box also closed. This was the second box, opened in June 1937, when the loop was extended.   *S.J.Dickson*

(Above) Morebath, 30th May 1964. The loop at Morebath had already been lifted by this date, when standard 3MT 2-6-2T No. **82001** coasts in with the 4.20pm Taunton-Barnstaple Junction train. *R.A.Lumber*

Morebath Junction, 30th August 1961. 43XX Class 2-6-0 No. **6390** uses the automatic tablet exchanger at the junction whilst passing on a Down train. The device was the GWR's version of the S&DJR Whitaker apparatus. *M.J.Fox*

(Below) Morebath Junction, 21st July 1961. 43XX Class 2-6-0 No. **7326** negotiates the junction with a train for Taunton. *M.J.Fox*

(Above) **Morebath Junction, 8th June 1961.** A 43XX Class 2-6-0 No. 7326 passing the junction bound for Bamstaple. *M.J.Fox*

Morebath Junction Halt, c.1950's. A view looking towards the junction. *Lens of Sutton*

(Below) **Western Region Timetable 17th June - 8th September 1963.** *Railway Study Centre*

Miles		am	am	am		pm	pm	pm G	pm F	am T	am T	am T	am	pm W	am T		pm		pm	pm	
62	London (Pad.) 61 dep	..	8 30	10 30	..	12 30	2 30	4 30	6 30	..	..	..	8 15	..	10 15	..	12 30	..	2 30	6 30	..
—	Taunton dep	8 5	11 15	pm 1 15	..	4 20	5 55	7 15	9 10	6 20	7 0	8 50	11 25	1 5	pm 1 57	..	4 25	..	5 55	9 10	..
6¼	Milverton	8 17	11 29	1 28	..	4 32	6 7	7 26	9 21	6 39	7 12	9 2	11 37	1 23	2 9	..	4 37	..	6 7	9 21	..
9¼	Wiveliscombe	8 25	11 37	1 35	..	4 39	6 15	7 33	9 28	6 39	7 19	9 10	11 44	1 31	2 17	..	4 45	..	6 15	9 28	..
14½	Venn Cross	8 36	11 48	1 46	..	4 51	6 26	7 44	9 39	..	7 30	9 21	11 55	..	..	..	4 56	..	6 26	9 39	..
17¾	Morebath	8 42	11 54	1 52	..	4 57	6 32	7 50	9 45	..	7 36	9 27	12 1	..	..	..	5 2	..	6 32	9 45	..
19¼	Morebath Junction Halt	8 47	11 59	1 57	..	5 2	6 37	7 58	9 49	..	..	9 32	12 6	..	..	..	5 7	..	6 37	9 49	..
21	Dulverton	8 53	12 5	2 5	..	5 10	6 44	8 4	9 55	7 6	7 48	9 38	12 12	2 8	2 50	..	5 13	..	6 44	9 55	..
24½	East Anstey	9 3	12 14	2 14	..	5 19	6 53	8 13	10 4	7 17	7 58	9 48	12 21	..	3 1	..	5 22	..	6 53	10 4	..
26¾	Yeo Mill Halt	9 8	12 19	2 19	..	5 24	6 58	8 18	10 9	..	..	9 53	12 26	..	..	..	5 27	..	7 4	10 15	..
30	Bishop's Nympton and	9 14	12 25	2 25	..	5 30	7 4	8 24	10 15	7 26	8 10	10 0	12 34	..	3 13	..	5 33	..	7 14	10 23	..
34¾	South Molton [Molland	9 23	12 33	2 33	..	5 39	7 14	8 32	10 23	7 38	8 18	10 13	12 43	2 36	3 23	..	5 42	..	7 23	10 32	..
37¾	Filleigh	9 32	12 42	2 45	..	5 48	7 23	8 41	10 32	7 48	8 28	10 24	12 52	..	3 32	..	5 58	..	7 30	10 39	..
40¾	Swimbridge	9 39	12 49	2 52	..	5 55	7 30	8 48	10 39	7 58	8 35	10 31	12 59	..	3 41	..	6 8	..	7 43	10 49	..
45¼	Barnstaple Junction arr	9 49	12 59	3 2	..	6 5	7 40	8 58	10 49	8 8	8 45	10 43	1 11	3 2	3 53	..	6 8	..	9 2	..	..
60¾	Ilfracombe arr	10 48	1 44	3 51	..	7 2	9 2	..	..	9 49	9 42	11 28	2 41	4 0	4 53	..	7 2	..	9 2	..	..

Exe Bridge, 30th August 1961. Between Morebath Junction and Dulverton, the line crossed the River Exe. Here 57XX Class 0-6-0PT No. **9670** is passing with the South Molton-Taunton pick up freight.

M.J.Fox

Dulverton, 22nd June 1963. 43XX Class 2-6-0 No. **7337** leaving with the 3.55pm Barnstaple-Taunton. In the bay platform 14XX 0-4-2T No. **1421** is waiting for departure with the Exe Valley auto-train for Exeter.

M.J.Fox

Dulverton, 10th October 1959. 43XX Class 2-6-0 No. **6398** enters the Up platform on the 2.25pm Barnstaple Victoria Road-Taunton goods, whilst the other platforms are occupied by SR Class N 2-6-0 No. **31846** on the 2.44pm ex-Taunton, and 4575 Class 2-6-2T No. **5524** on the 3.42pm auto-train to Exeter. The engine was only equipped with this apparatus for the last two years of its life. *P.W.Gray*

Dulverton, c.1959. A view showing the platform that the Exe Valley trains used. The turntable shown was used for turning the 14XX Class locos on the Exe Valley trains. In 1910 the new layout of the yard came into use and the turntable, which had been left in its original place, was now accessed from the Barnstaple end of the station. It was taken out of use in April 1964. *S.J.Dickson*

2nd-SINGLE SINGLE-2nd
Dulverton to
Dulverton   Dulverton
Bath Spa   Bath Spa
BATH SPA
via Bristol
For alternative routes see book of routes
(W)   18/0   Fare   18/0   (W)
For conditions see over   For conditions see over
828   828

Dulverton, c.1950s. 4575 Class 2-6-2T No. **5525** passes on an Up branch freight, whilst the Exe Valley auto-train stands in the bay platform. The signal box was at that time still a wooden structure; later in BR days it was rebuilt with a brick base.

Lens of Sutton

East Anstey, 7th July 1962. 43XX Class 2-6-0 No. **7337** arriving on the 8.35am SO Ilfracombe-Manchester train.

P.W.Gray

(Above) **Yeo Mill Halt, 7th July 1962.** 43XX Class 2-6-0 No. **6372** approaching the halt on the 9.20am Ilfracombe-Taunton.
P.W.Gray

(Below) **Yeo Mill Halt, c.1959.** In the area that the halt served there was only a small community, with old fashioned names Cuckoo Farm, Ruggleypitt and Bottreaux Mill. The halt was only opened on 27th June 1932 and as could be expected the traffic returns were low.
S.J.Dickson

(Above) **Yeo Mill Halt, c.1959.** The notice board at the approach to the halt was still in situ at this date with the original enamel sign of the Great Western Railway. The halt was, in terms of the branch, relatively new having opened on the 27th June 1932.
S.J.Dickson

Bishops Nympton and Molland, 24th September 1966. A week before closure, a 3-car DMU provides the 5.55pm Barnstaple-Taunton service.

R.A.Lumber

South Molton, 27th June 1964. 43XX Class 2-6-0 No. **6345** is the power for a Saturday Ilfracombe-Cardiff train. The Down platform road at that stage was signalled for either direction of running.

R.A.Lumber

Filleigh Viaduct, September 1962. An unidentified 43XX Class locomotive on a passenger working is seen here crossing the girders of the viaduct.
S.J.Dickson

Filleigh Viaduct, c.1925. An unidentified Dean Goods 0-6-0 and goods train crossing Castle Hill Viaduct. The similarity of construction with Tone
A. Halls
Viaduct will be noted.

Filleigh Viaduct, September 1962. The viaduct was built on stone pillars giving a maximum height above the valley floor of 94ft. It had six spans.
S.J.Dickson

G. W. R.

FILLEIGH

(Below) Filleigh Station, c.1961. A view looking towards Barnstaple. The signal box shown was the new box opened in June 1937 when the new Down loop was brought into use. The old box that was situated on the Up platform was taken out of use and demolished. *S.J.Dickson*

Swimbridge, 27th June 1964. LMS Class 2MT 2-6-2T No. **41216**, a substitute engine provided by Barnstaple Junction shed (72E), on the 1.11pm Barnstaple-Taunton train.   *R.A.Lumber*

Barnstaple East Junction, c.1930. 4575 Class 2-6-2T No. **5502** soon after leaving Barnstaple on a Taunton train.   *A.Halls*

(Above) Barnstaple Victoria Road, June 1960. A view of the station buildings taken from the end loading dock. Little had changed at this end of the station from the day it was built in 1876. What is lacking in this view is the plethora of enamel signs that once adorned both the railings and end of the station building. The station closed to passenger traffic on the 13th June 1960. *S.J.Dickson*

(Centre) Barnstaple Victoria Road, June 1961. By this date, with the demise of passenger services, the station was being used for goods services only. The view shows the approach to the station, the goods shed on the left and on the right the curved extension of the original platform canopy which had been walled in to form a store. By this date all the signals had been removed after the signal box closed in June 1960. *S.J.Dickson*

(Left) Barnstaple Victoria Road, c.1930. Bulldog Class 4-4-0 No. 3453 *Seagull* on the turntable at Barnstaple GWR loco shed. *A.Halls*

British Transport Commission (S)

BARNSTAPLE

PLATFORM TICKET 2d.
Available one hour on day of issue only.
Not valid in trains. Not transferable.
To be given up when leaving platform.
For conditions see over

2897

Tiverton-Morebath Junction

The northern section of the Exe Valley branch from Tiverton to Morebath Junction, the section recorded in this book, was actually opened shortly before the Exeter-Tiverton section, and was strictly the Tiverton and North Devon Railway. The only station on this section served its only intermediate town, Bampton (Devon). The parentheses in the name the GWR used were necessary because they had another Bampton station in Oxfordshire, on the Fairford branch.

Bampton reflected the B&E style station with an "H" plan and central porch found elsewhere in our area, although the B&E had been absorbed by the GWR before this line was constructed and the buildings were ostensibly designed by a local architect. Similar buildings were built south of Tiverton at Cadeleigh, Thorverton etc. Tiverton station itself was grander, particularly in its stone staircases up to the footbridge. Later halts were opened at Cove (1923) and Bolham (1928).

Exe Valley trains were normally formed of a pair of auto-trailers powered by the appropriately equipped 14XX 0-4-2Ts, these being supplied by Exeter shed (83C). When non-fitted engines were in use, e.g. 57XX pannier tanks on occasion, they had of course to run round. Not all trains ran through from Exeter to Dulverton; some terminated at Tiverton, or Bampton.

By 1960 no Exe Valley goods service ran above Tiverton; if traffic had to be handled at Bampton this was done from the Devon & Somerset end. The returning South Molton-Taunton pick-up goods had a lengthy break at Dulverton around lunchtime and ran down to Bampton during this interval if required. Closure of the line took place during 1963.

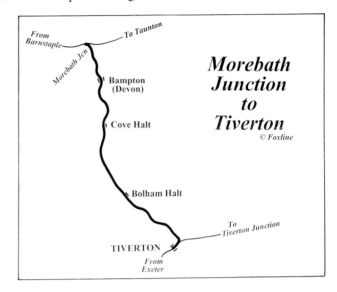

Morebath Junction to Tiverton
© Foxline

Bampton (Devon), 16th March 1963. 14XX Class 0-4-2T No. **1450** waiting departure on the 3.20pm Bampton-Exeter auto-train. This view shows particularly well the "H" shaped floorplan which was similar to many B&E station buildings, often with the central space on the platform side glazed to provide a shelter.

P.W.Gray

Bampton (Devon), 28th September 1963. A week before closure a North British Loco type 2 Diesel-Hydraulic No. **D6318** is being used as motive-power for the two auto-trailers. This was a rehearsal for the heavier "last day" trains put on to cope with the crowds.　　　　　*Hugh Ballantyne*

Bampton (Devon), 8th August 1962. 14XX Class 0-4-2T No. **1462** arriving on the 4.25pm Exeter-Bampton auto-train.　　　　　*M.J.Fox*

(Above) Cove Halt, 15th June 1963. 14XX Class 0-4-2T No. **1450** propelling the 3.20pm Bampton-Exeter out of the halt. In this view the scene looks one of peace and tranquility but it was not. The quarry buildings as can be seen in the next photograph produced much clatter and dust.

P.W.Gray

Cove Halt, c.1950's. Looking towards Morebath Junction. Just past the crossing was the siding on the left hand side of the track which served the quarry, the buildings being seen in the distance. This siding had a capacity of three wagons! *Lens of Sutton*

Bolham Halt c.1950's. Looking towards Morebath Junction. The halt was opened on the 24th April 1928 and was at the village of Bolham. Near by was the Heathcoat Amory family home of 'Knightshayes'. This family boasted a long connection with both industry and public life in Tiverton.

Lens of Sutton

(Below) Bolham Halt, 18th August 1962. 14XX Class 0-4-2T No. **1450** leaving with the strengthened 9.45am Exeter-Dulverton. *P.W.Gray*

Tiverton, 26th September 1964. A view of Tiverton station showing the Tiverton Junction auto-train beneath the footbridge. More to the point however is the fact that the station was now only two weeks from closure.

M.J.Fox

Tiverton, 29th September 1962. Not in fact operating as an auto-train, 57XX Class 0-6-0PT No. **3659** and two trailers approach the station, forming the 9.25am Dulverton-Exeter train.

M.J.Fox

Tiverton

Rarely can a rural location have enjoyed train services such as Tiverton, totalling some fifty weekday arrivals and departures. The Exe Valley accounted for half of these, the remainder connecting the town with Tiverton Junction some 5 miles away on the B & E route. This comprehensive arrangement, including summer Sunday operation between Exeter and Tiverton, remained in place until withdrawal of the Exeter/Dulverton passenger services in the autumn of 1963. Passenger train connections with the main line at Tiverton Junction would continue for another twelve months, until this service too was withdrawn (5th October 1964). This, the remaining rail link to the town, for goods traffic, lasted until May 1967.

Tiverton, 10tb August 1961. The station from the east, with 14XX Class 0-4-2T No. **1466** propelling the 3.42pm Dulverton-Exeter train, 57XX Class 0-6-0PT No. **9765** on the Exeter-Dulverton 3.21pm, and 14XX No. **1471** shunting.
Hugh Ballantyne

Tiverton, 29th September 1962. In the course of its shunting activities, 57XX Class 0-6-0PT No. **8783** collects the vans from the rear of the Tiverton Junction train standing in its bay platform. This is the same train which is depicted arriving in one of the other photographs.
M.J.Fox

Tiverton, 26th September 1964. 14XX Class 0-4-2T No. **1450** propelling the 10.25am Tiverton Junction-Tiverton into the station. The Exe Valley service having ceased the previous autumn, the train can use the through platform instead of its bay.   *M.J.Fox*

Tiverton, 29th September 1962. The 9.41am Tiverton-Tiverton Junction auto-train arriving at Tiverton, propelled by 14XX Class 0-4-2T No. **1451** which is also hauling two fitted vans.   *M.J.Fox*

Tiverton-Tiverton Junction

This line was the original rail connection to Tiverton. It was opened from the broad gauge Bristol & Exeter main line in 1848 and converted to standard gauge in 1884 on construction of the Exe Valley line.

The passenger service in latter years was a shuttle auto-train connecting with the main line; the celebrated "Tivvy Bumper". There was only one intermediate halt, at Halberton. Clearances were ample enough for the waiting shelter at Halberton Halt (opened in 1927) to be located under a bridge, for it had been planned as a double-track line. The clearances were also obvious nearby, where the line burrowed under an aqueduct of the Grand Western Canal. This was a predecessor of the railway, planned to link the Bristol and English Channels, by connecting the Bridgwater Canal with Exeter, and with a branch to Tiverton. In the event, only the Taunton-Tiverton section was completed and, like the other canals in this area, fell into railway hands.

The intermediate halt at Halberton had no goods facilities, but the line did see some goods traffic, in local freight workings from Exeter to Taunton via Tiverton.

The line closed in 1964, twelve months after the withdrawal of the Exe Valley service to Tiverton. The Railway Gallery of Tiverton Museum holds many photographs and other relics of the local lines, by far the largest of which is 14XX 0-4-2T No 1442.

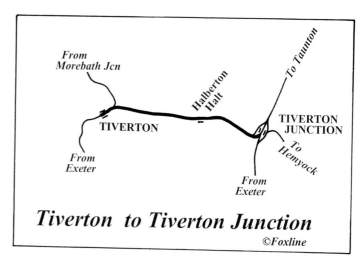

Tiverton to Tiverton Junction

©Foxline

Halberton Halt, 31st August 1961. 14XX Class 0-4-2T No. **1420** leaving with the 10.55am Tiverton-Tiverton Junction auto-train. The line was originally both broad gauge and planned for double track, hence the ample space under the bridge where the halt was built. *M.J.Fox*

Halberton, 14th June 1958. 14XX Class 0-4-2T No. **1405** passing under the Grand Western Canal aqueduct with a Tiverton-Tiverton Junction train.
M.J.Fox

Halberton Halt was a scheduled stop on all services between Tiverton and Tiverton Junction. It was 5 minutes from the Junction in the twelve minute journey. During the last period of operation in 1964 there were thirteen trains in each direction with additional ones on Tuesday, presumably for Tiverton market. The one and only Sunday train, from Tiverton to Exeter, called here at 9.4 in the evening. There was not a balanced working.

(Below) Halberton Halt, 21st December 1963. 14XX Class 0-4-2T No. **1466** departing for Tiverton Junction. *M.J.Fox*

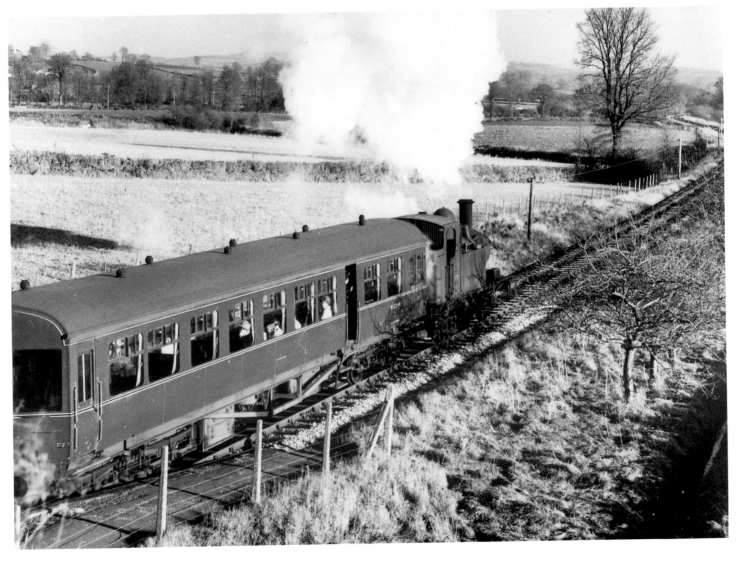

Tiverton Junction – Hemyock

The Hemyock branch, or Culm Valley Light Railway, was opened in 1876 as a standard gauge branch serving the upper Culm Valley, built cheaply to standard gauge, and operated by the Great Western. It was indeed very much a Light Railway, winding its way around and between the fields. The quaint and distinctive little station buildings at Uffculme, Culmstock and Hemyock were a standard design of the line's engineer, Arthur Pain. Amazingly their closest relatives, with the same half- timbering and brick infill were on his narrow-gauge Southwold Railway in Suffolk. In addition to the stations, halts were opened at Coldharbour in 1929 and Whitehall in 1933.

The pattern of train services was determined very much by the principal traffic, which was not passengers, but milk from the large dairy at Hemyock. The light axle loading and tight curvature severely restricted both loco and rolling stock. Another restricting factor was the extremely short run-round loops at the intermediate stations (extension of the loop at Hemyock itself was an improvement undertaken about 1930).

Two 0-6-0T locos, numbers 1376 and 1377 were designed to operate the line, but soon found unsuitable. Thereafter until 1932 a variety of small 2-4-0T designs were tried, these having originated on the South Devon, Liskeard & Looe, Princes Risborough & Watlington, and Cambrian Railways. Then one of the new updated 0-4-2Ts was tried, and these ruled the branch for the rest of its existence. The first one used was a 58XX (non-auto-fitted) example but afterwards 48XX (14XX) auto fitted engines. Not that an auto-coach ever appeared on the Culm Valley - they would have been far too long for the curves - but because all Exeter's other 0-4-2T duties were on auto-trains, and so permanently earmarking a particular engine for the Culm Valley branch was avoided.

Bogie carriages had to be short; when all the old Dean vehicles had worn out a pair of 54ft length Barry Railway coaches built in 1921 were kept until about 1962 when they were condemned and replaced by a pair of 52ft Thompson coaches transferred from the ER. The train normally consisted of one of these brake 3rd coaches and as many milk tankers as were required or could be run round at Hemyock. The one train which didn't handle milk was a short working which, instead, acted as a mixed for Uffculme, except on Saturdays when it continued to Culmstock. It should be pointed out that a passenger/milk train did not constitute a mixed; the tanks were passenger-rated vehicles. When a due mixed was run the wagons were marshalled between the coach and a goods brake van.

Although passenger services were withdrawn in 1963 milk trains continued to operate until 1975, motive power being a Class 03 200hp Diesel shunter. However, for as long as one steam engine was still maintained at Tiverton Junction for the SuX 'Tivvy Bumper", the shunter might be failed on a Sunday and steam substituted for the benefit of people in the know.

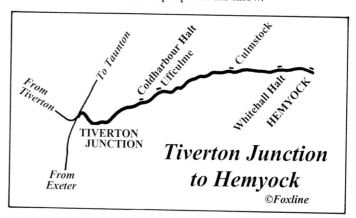

Tiverton Junction to Hemyock

©Foxline

Tiverton Junction, 23rd December 1963. After withdrawal of the Culm Valley passenger service the goods traffic was worked by a 200hp Diesel shunter; even so, steam might be substituted from time to time. On such an occasion, 14XX Class 0-4-2T No. **1450** is departing "engine and brake van" down the branch.   *M.J.Fox*

BRITISH RYS. (Western Region)
(4237)
TO
TIVERTON
(DEVON)

(Above) Coldharbour Halt, 3rd November 1962. This halt was opened primarily in order to serve workers at the Coldharbour textile mill seen in the background. The mill had been purchased in 1797 by Fox Bros. The Foxe's were a Quaker family and a very considerate and compassionate employers. During the building of the branch Thomas Fox had subscribed £2,000 in ordinary shares to the company. When in May 1877 the siding had been added, for the use of Fox Bros. and the public, it was Fox Bros. who paid for the signals. 14XX Class 0-4-2T No. **1421** is arriving with the 11.25am Tiverton Junction-Culmstock train.   *P.W.Gray*

Coldharbour Halt, c.1950's. A view looking towards Tiverton Junction.
Lens of Sutton

Uffculme, 22nd June 1963. 14XX Class 0-4-2T No. **1450** arriving with the 9.20am Tiverton Junction-Hemyock, comprising one of the pair of ER Thompson coaches which replaced the Barry Railway pair for the last few years of the branch's existence. The view shows well the Arthur Pain station building in almost original condition.

M.J.Fox

Uffculme, c.1947. A view looking towards Hemyock. The number of 0-4-2T No. **4827** gives a clue to the date, as these locos were renumbered into the 14XX series in 1947 when 48XX numbers were allotted to oil-burning conversions of 28XX Class 2-8-0s.

Lens of Sutton

Culmstock, 8th August 1962. 14XX Class 0-4-2T No. **1450** departing with the 2.45pm Hemyock-Tiverton Junction. Opening and closing the level crossing gates on this line was normally left to the train crew.   *M.J.Fox*

(Below left) Culmstock, c.1959. Here 14XX Class 0-4-2T No. **1440** is standing in the station with a Tiverton Junction-Hemyock train. The composition of this passenger train; loco, milk tankers, and Barry Railway coach is absolutely typical.   *M.J.Fox*

(Below) Culmstock, 31st September 1961. 14XX Class 0-4-2T No. **1466** stands at the platform with the Tiverton Junction - Hemyock train.   *M.J.Fox*

(Above) Whitehall Halt, 4th November 1961. The loco fireman opens the crossing gates for the 3.00pm train from Hemyock.   *P.W.Gray*

Whitehall Halt, 22nd June 1963. 14XX Class 0-4-2T No. **1450** draws into the halt with the 10.30am Hemyock-Tiverton Junction train. Whitehall Halt was opened by the GWR on the 27th February 1933 with a view to further traffic from the area. Just over thirty years later, on 7th September 1963 the halt was closed to passengers and goods. The short siding held only three wagons and it was a requirement that no locomotives were permitted to use it. During September and October of that year the siding was lifted.   *M.J.Fox*

Hemyock, 11th May 1957. This view with 14XX Class 0-4-2T No. **1429** and train illustrates the proximity of the river, and also the milk depot across the road behind the station. The siding into the dairy provided the main revenue of the branch.   *M.J.Fox*

(Below) **Hemyock, 3rd November 1962.** 14XX Class 0-4-2T No. **1421** drawing to a halt on the 1.42pm from Tiverton Junction. The train does not include any empty milk tankers, but a number are standing in the yard. As originally built, the station building at Hemyock proved too small for the facilities needed, and was twice rebuilt. The second modification was the concrete block extension which is very obvious in this picture.   *P.W.Gray*